Organizational Change

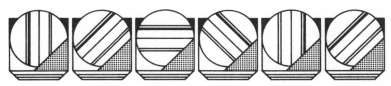

Management Applications Series

Alan C. Filley, University of Wisconsin, Madison
Series Editor

Performance in Organizations: Determinants and Appraisal
L. L. Cummings, University of Wisconsin, Madison
Donald P. Schwab, University of Wisconsin, Madison

Leadership and Effective Management
Fred E. Fiedler, University of Washington
Martin M. Chemers, University of Utah

Managing by Objectives
Anthony P. Raia, University of California, Los Angeles

Organizational Change: Techniques and Applications
Newton Margulies, University of California, Irvine
John C. Wallace, University of California, Irvine

Interpersonal Conflict Resolution
Alan C. Filley, University of Wisconsin, Madison

Analysis of Organization Design
Elmer Burack, Illinois Institute of Technology

Program Planning
Andre Delbecq, University of Wisconsin, Madison

Organizational Change

techniques & applications

Newton Margulies and John Wallace

Graduate School of Administration
University of California, Irvine

Scott, Foresman and Company
Glenview, Illinois   Brighton, England

To Gordon, Steven, and Jeffrey
and
Andrea and Tracy

Library of Congress Catalogue Number: 72–96498
ISBN: 0–673–07761–6.

Regional offices of Scott, Foresman and Company are located in Dallas,
Texas; Glenview, Illinois; Oakland, New Jersey; Palo Alto, California;
Tucker, Georgia; and Brighton, England.

Foreword

The Management Applications Series is concerned with the application of contemporary research, theory, and techniques. There are many excellent books at advanced levels of knowledge, but there are few which address themselves to the application of such knowledge. The authors in this series are uniquely qualified for this purpose, since they are all scholars who have experience in implementing change in real organizations through the methods they write about.

Each book treats a single topic in depth. Where the choice is between presenting many approaches briefly or a single approach thoroughly, we have opted for the latter. Thus, after reading the book, the student or practitioner should know how to apply the methodology described.

Selection of topics for the series was guided by contemporary relevance to management practice, and by the availability of an author qualified as an expert, yet able to write at a basic level of understanding. No attempt is made to cover all management methods, nor is any sequence implied in the series, although the books do complement one another. For example, change methods might fit well with managing by objectives.

The books in this series may be used in several ways. They may be used to supplement textbooks in basic courses on management, organizational behavior, personnel, or industrial psychology/sociology. Students appreciate the fact that the material is immediately applicable. Practicing managers will want to use individual books to increase their skills, either through self study or in connection with management development programs, inside or outside the organization.

Alan C. Filley

Preface

"There is nothing so practical as a good theory," Kurt Lewin is reputed to have said. We rather like Lewin's remark, but we know of one equally true. *There is nothing so practical as a good practice.* Strict logicians' objections to the contrary, we find both notions correct and, in fact, complementary. Although our book is concerned with theory, it emphasizes practice. In particular, the practice of the techniques of organizational change. In this book we have tried to provide information concerning the most recent developments in organizational change, drawn from applied behavioral science. Our concern is with analysis, but with analysis that leads to *action*. For it is equally true that there is nothing so *impractical* as a good theory that leads nowhere.

In the course of our studies of organizational change, we have been impressed by how many people love to *talk* about change. The rhetoric of change is everywhere. This is quite understandable, as change is a fascinating topic, especially for discussion. But as both of us have had occasion to say to managers willing to change, but who don't know where to begin, "The way to change your organization is to change your organization." This may sound silly, but from our perspective, there is more than a grain of truth in it.

Planned organizational change requires effort and imagination. It isn't an easy business. Aside from effort and imagination, it requires knowledge and understanding. And it is our conviction that it is the latter two factors that are often missing. Even in organizations that are willing and ready for change, change will not magically happen. Somebody must know how to make it happen, initiate it, manage it, and see that it occurs smoothly and effectively.

Thus, our book is dedicated to those managers of vision and those perceptive students of administration who see the necessity for planned change as perhaps the most critical problem facing modern, complex organizational systems.

Newton Margulies
John Wallace

Contents

Introduction

1

We who live in this latter part of the twentieth century are witnesses to remarkable, rapid, and even, for some of us, overwhelming change. While many historical periods can be rightfully called transitional eras, none can match the present in terms of the nature, frequency, and magnitude of the changes with which people must cope. The bold advances of modern technologies, the rapid expansion of the scientific information pool, and the profound questioning of social structures, values, and institutions have been evident to even the most casual observer of the past several decades. Whether we approve of such rapid change or not is truly beside the point. In the final analysis, we must learn to live with it. More correctly, we must learn to *manage* such change if we are to live out our lives with some degree of contentment, meaningfulness, and useful purpose.

For the modern organization, the lesson is clear. Given the facts of rapid, unplanned change, a static organization cannot survive. Yesterday's successes mean very little in a world of rapidly changing markets, consumers, products, values, life-styles, and so forth. In order to survive, modern organizations must devise means of continuous self-renewal. They must be able to recognize when it is necessary to change, and above all, they must possess the competency to bring about change when it is required. Unfortunately, while competency in technological matters has steadily increased, expertise in dealing with the organization as a complex social system has lagged far behind. One is even tempted to conclude that modern organizations know far more about resisting and preventing change than they do about initiating and facilitating it. This need no longer be the case. Although in its

1

beginning stages, a technology of organizational change does exist. Moreover, it can be taught and learned like any other body of technological information.

In the following pages, we have tried to present clearly and simply some major ideas and techniques concerning the initiation and facilitation of change in organizations. Our focus is clearly that of *applied behavioral science.* Our emphasis is upon *behavior change* of organization members. Among the various possible approaches to organizational change, ours is clearly that of a "people" approach. For the most part, we have not concerned ourselves with approaches which emphasize change in such things as the administrative structure, technology, or the work flow process. It is not that we regard these as unimportant or see them as unrelated to the problem. Obviously, the initial thrust of any change effort could very well be concerned with any of these, people, administrative structure, technology, or work flow. In the final analysis, however, all organizational change efforts, regardless of initial focus, must take account of the fact that *people are being called upon to do things differently.* In this sense, behavior change is involved in all organizational change efforts. Any organizational change effort which does not take into account the necessity for individual behavior change is likely to prove unnecessarily difficult or, in some cases, to fail completely.

Let us illustrate with some examples. A production organization introduces a new work technology without consideration of the fact that the change in technology now requires people to work in collaborative team settings. Management is surprised to find that productivity decreases sharply after the introduction of the change. In this case, management failed to recognize that effective team performance does not occur spontaneously but must be systematically planned and developed.

Consider another example. Sweeping changes in educational method and the content of instruction are proposed at the level of a state legislature. Despite the fact that such changes become law, few substantial changes occur at the level of the classroom, the critical point in the educational services delivery system. Nobody has taken into account the seemingly obvious fact that individual teacher attitudes and behaviors must also change if the intent of the legislature is to be carried out. Once again, such changes in teacher behavior do not occur spontaneously but are the outcome of thoughtful in-service teacher retraining programs.

These and many other possible examples illustrate our main

point. It is difficult, if not impossible, to conceive of any significant change in a functioning organization that does not require changes in the behavior of the persons who cause it to function.

This book, then, is concerned with behavior change. The techniques we describe in the following pages are, in our opinion, useful in two ways. First, they can be employed directly where "people" change is the initial focus of the change effort. Secondly, they can be used as integral and supportive parts of change programs in which the *initial* concern is not with individual behavior but with some aspect of structure or technology.

A BRIEF OVERVIEW OF THE BOOK

Let us consider briefly what the reader can expect to know after a careful reading of our book. The book is designed to do the following:

1) Examine the range of techniques drawn from applied behavioral science and considered useful in *planned* organizational change programs.

2) Present these techniques simply and in detail enough to give both managers and advanced students of administrative sciences a clear understanding of them.

3) Examine the factors that determine intelligent *choice* among the various techniques while taking into account such factors as appropriateness for given organizational problems, contexts, and costs. We assume that each of the techniques is useful for some purposes and not for others. None are "magical" cures for all organizational difficulties; all have specific constraints.

4) Present the theory underlying these techniques with simplicity and clarity so that the reader can grasp their origins, meanings, and implications. It is not, however, our intent to present exhaustive discussions of related theory or to examine critically and in detail the empirical research bearing upon them.

With the exception of Chapter 2, which is explicitly concerned with theory, this text concerns itself with specific change techniques. We have made no attempt to integrate the several chapters into a single, all-encompassing, unified model of change. The reader is cautioned not to expect full transitions from one chapter to the next but to approach each chapter as a separate essay on a selected topic.

Chapter 2 presents the underlying dimensions of theories about change. While this chapter does not concern itself with the particulars of actual techniques, it should be read carefully for an understanding of the issues that underlie the theories. Most importantly, this discussion should make the manager aware of the *choices* available to him in constructing his own belief system about the ways effective change can be brought about in his organization.

The remaining chapters of the book are centered about particular techniques and the bodies of theory from which they are derived. Chapter 3 takes up the important topic of action research in the context of the organization. This chapter shows how data relevant to the change process can be gathered and applied in a particular organization, and shows how such data can be utilized effectively in an ongoing program.

In Chapter 4, the organization is presented as a social learning system, one in which various social processes are always present to produce learning and, hence, changes in behavior. From our perspective, it is valuable for the manager to understand the organization from the social learning viewpoint if only to gain a greater appreciation of the organization as it exists. More important, however, is our conviction that the manager knowledgeable about social learning processes can *intervene* in them actively and use them effectively for organizational change.

Chapter 5 discusses the relatively recent innovation of laboratory method. Perhaps more than any other method of change, the T-group has attracted widespread interest and controversy. And perhaps more than any other method, the T-group has been the most poorly understood and improperly applied. In this chapter an effort is made to clarify the ways in which the T-group can be employed, but we have also tried to show that many variants of the laboratory method exist besides the basic T-group and that conditions do exist in the organization that demand discriminating and selective application of this range of techniques.

Chapter 6 briefly presents the elementary concepts of role theory and then shows how techniques derived from it can be used in the context of the organization. In addition to discussion of such things as role-playing, role analysis, and role-training, we consider a little-practiced technique that appears to have considerable promise, that of *role prescription.*

The important topics of *teams* and *team development* are discussed at length in Chapter 7, while Chapter 8 takes up the problem of intergroup conflict and relationships within an organization. In both of these chapters, the emphasis is upon the group and group interaction rather than individual behavior *per se.* Chapter 9 concerns the use of internal consulting teams and shows how an organization can develop consultative talent from resources within itself.

In essence, then, we see the problem of organizational change as critical. Organizations must learn to adjust effectively to meet the unstable demands of internal and external reality. Managers who see themselves as change agents and who know how to function effectively in this capacity are clearly among the most valuable members of the organization. It is our hope that this book will assist them in developing the necessary knowledge to cope with the many problems associated with organizational change.

Let us begin then with a discussion of the theoretical issues. When we consider the problems inherent in changing the behavior of organizational members, what underlying dimensions become apparent? The next chapter addresses itself to this important question.

Critical Dimensions

of Change

2

Each of us, in a very real sense, has a "theory" of change. We need not be formally labeled "psychologist," "change agent," "manager," or "consultant" to possess opinions and notions about how people change and are changed. Even those persons of a practical bent who do not wish to be bothered by "irrelevant, abstract, and vague theories" can be shown to possess theories of their own. To be sure, these "naive" theories of behavior change are often implicit and poorly verbalized. Nonetheless they do exist and often influence the ways in which their holders act. The supervisor who blocks a pay raise for a subordinate may very well believe that changed behavior results from punishment. The top executive who encourages participation in decision-making at all organizational levels may believe that this is a way to change members' commitment and loyalty in a positive direction. These and many other possible examples illustrate the importance of naive theories of change. Of course, in addition to the informal theories that each of us holds, there are numerous *formal* theories of behavior change as well. On careful examination, it is evident that these formal theories vary as much as do the naive theories. They vary greatly in degree of sophistication, from those that are indistinguishable from the simple theories of everyday life to the highly complex and precisely articulated statements of the behavioral scientist.

In short, there are many theories of behavior change, both

formal and informal. Each appears to build upon different assumptions and to possess different ways of talking about and representing events. Despite such apparent diversity, however, it is possible to reduce these many differences to a few important *dimensions* along which most theories of change vary. What are these general dimensions? A discussion of this question will have two important outcomes. First, it will enable us to reduce unnecessary complexity, and second, it will assist the reader to make explicit his own ideas of how change can be brought about.

INDIVIDUAL VERSUS SOCIALLY ORIENTED CONCEPTIONS

Some theories of change make little of the social networks into which each of us is born and, with the exception of the rare recluse, live out our years. Traditional *psychodynamic* theories of change, drawn largely from psychoanalytic thought, most typically present the problem of change as a largely *internal* affair. In psychodynamic accounts of human personality and personality change, emphasis is placed upon events inside the person. One's behavior is seen as determined by complex internal forces, unconscious motivations, conflicts, and defense systems. In such systems of thought, changes in overt behavior cannot be expected until these many aspects of inner life are therapeutically altered. For the most part, the social reality of the person is not emphasized either in bringing about change or in the *maintenance* of change once it has begun to occur. The classical situations for change are those suggested by the doctor-patient, therapist-client, and expert-novice relationships (Menninger, 1958). Although not necessarily the case, the change situation is essentially one in which an authority, by reason of his training, expertise, and credentials, is not only granted legitimacy but is expected to bring about changes in the willing consumer of his services.

In contrast to individually oriented change theories, social theories of change emphasize the importance of the many interpersonal, group, organizational, societal, and even cultural factors which can and do exert powerful influences over individual behavior. *Role* accounts of behavior change, for example, do not separate the individual from the social structure in which he is most typically found (Kahn, et al., 1964). The individual actor is seen as occupying a *position* in a social structure and that position is seen as carrying numerous *expectations* for behavior. In some circumstances, the actor is forced to deal with contradictory expectations for the position that he occupies, while in others, the expectations may be ambiguous. In still other circumstances, the actor simply may not possess the skills necessary for adequate role performance, but whatever the situation, his behavior is seen as embedded in a matrix of social factors and any attempt to change it must take into account the total social situation in which he operates.

Socially oriented change theorists are much more likely to utilize the context of the *group,* and the sensitivity training group and the gestalt encounter group are two relatively recent innovations in the technology of change. The group context for change permits a variety of experiences that the two-person expert-client relationship lacks. First of all, in the context of the group, the person must deal with a variety of other individuals. As a consequence, the full range of his coping and defensive strategies for dealing with others is more likely to become evident. Secondly, *feedback* about his behavior may be gained more easily from a number of participant-observers than from a single person. It may be quite valuable for the person to discover that his behavior does not affect all persons in the same manner. And equally valuable to find, in some instances, that his behavior evokes the *same* feelings and counteractions from virtually everyone with whom he interacts. While it may be possible to minimize and ignore feedback from one other person, it is quite difficult to dismiss uniform and consistent perceptions from as many as ten other observers. Finally, the group context for change permits the person to learn by *observing* the interactive styles of others. It is not at all unusual in group change contexts to have persons learn much about their own behavior by intently watching the ways in which other human beings attempt to cope with those difficult aspects of existence which perplex us all.

Change theorists who focus upon social factors differ from individual theorists in still another important way. It is now fairly evident that even the best of change efforts cannot be expected to succeed if attention is not paid to the *maintenance* of changed behaviors. Of what worth is a change process that permits the person to be fearless and confident in the presence of his therapist but miserable in his real context? Or how valuable is a sensitivity training experience that "turns people on" for a weekend away from the organization but whose effects are not detectable two weeks later back on the job? Quite recently, change theorists have begun to examine the necessity for supportive changes in the life situation of the person as an integral part of the change process. In the context of the organization, this clearly implies that individual change, if it is to be maintained, must be accompanied by some degree of social system change as well. Socially oriented change theorists have been much readier to recognize the necessity for environmental supports in the change process than have those theorists oriented primarily toward the individual. It seems quite evident to us that ample evidence now exists for one to believe firmly that the neglect of either social or individual factors in both the initiation and maintenance of change is unwise.

MINIMAL CHANGE VERSUS MAXIMAL CHANGE

Change theorists differ with regard to the extent of the changes which must take place before behavior can in any specific sense be changed. There are those theorists who seem to believe that the entire personality must first be restructured. Others adopt a more simplistic view and argue that it is possible to change certain aspects of behavior *simply by changing those aspects alone.* It is perhaps easiest to understand this controversy by using the analogy of symptom and disease, one which certain change theorists have, in fact, employed. The argument goes that overt behavior is often a "symptom" of some underlying disease process, and as the physician would not dream of treating the outward manifestations of cancer with topical creams, neither should the change agent attempt to alter directly the overt behavior of his client. The behavior, it is argued, is but a reflection of some deeper, more serious matter. Quite recently, these long-standing assumptions drawn from the symptom-disease model for therapeutic action have been challenged by change agents employing techniques drawn from studies of human *learning and social-psychological* theory (Wolpe, 1958; Bandura and Walters, 1963). Ample evidence from several contexts now exists to show that certain aspects of behavior can be altered by changing those aspects *alone* in a direct fashion. Change techniques derived from both traditional and social learning theories have been successfully applied to the control and change of such diverse behaviors as overeating, refusal to eat, smoking, irrational fears, children's behavior problems, and adult sexual problems. Most importantly, it has been demonstrated quite convincingly that these changes in behavior can be brought about without attempting to modify the total personality of the person.

HISTORICAL RECONSTRUCTIVE APPROACHES VERSUS CONTEMPORARY ANALYSIS

Change theories differ in the emphasis placed upon historical analysis of the person versus analysis of the contemporary life situation. These differences are a logical outcome of the assumptions made about the importance of early life experiences in determining the adult personality. Psychoanalytic personality theory, for example, assumes that the broad outlines of personality are developed quite early in the life of the person. Moreover, this body of thought assumes that it is these very early life experiences (before the age of five) which are prepotent in determining adult behavior patterns.

In contrast, the *sensitivity training* and gestalt *encounter group* formats for change require that the person seeking change concentrate on the *here and now*. In such a setting, the person is asked to focus upon his present feelings and behaviors. Analysis of past events is quite typically discouraged.

STRUCTURED VERSUS UNSTRUCTURED CHANGE SETTINGS

Learning situations in which change is discussed and experimented with vary in the degrees of their structures. Various learning theory approaches to change, for example, are typically quite structured with very clear prescriptions given for the behavior of both the change agent and the person seeking change. The person may be asked to perform detailed exercises involving carefully arranged sequences of behavior in response to highly controlled conditions established by the change agent.

Quite the opposite may take place in a sensitivity training group where the situation is left deliberately unstructured by the trainer or leader. Under these conditions of minimal structuring by a nonauthoritarian leader, members of the sensitivity training group are thrown back upon their own resources in dealing with an ambiguous social situation, one in which problems arising from minimal social structuring must be coped with.

FEELINGS VERSUS INTELLECT

All change theories are, of course, concerned with emotion. Once again, however, differences in the extent to which feelings are given prominence in the change process are found among the various theories. Some theorists place considerable emphasis upon the role of reason and logic in producing individual change. Albert Ellis (1962), for example, has devised a form of psychotherapy which he calls *rational therapy*. For Ellis, the patient must examine his *implicit* major and minor premises and the faulty conclusions which flow from them if change is to be expected. Ellis is led to this position by his conviction that what actually happens to a person is not important; what he *tells* himself about what is happening is, for in the telling, he may very well come up with extraordinary conclusions and irrational projections into the future from his unexamined assumptions.

Perhaps the extreme of naked emotion in the service of individual change is provided by the psychotherapy devised recently by A. Janov (1970) and called *primal therapy*. The change process, according to Janov, is only successful when the person can relive the traumatic events experienced in infancy and early childhood. These events are reexperienced through the *primal scream*, an emotional reenactment of the painful experiences in the lives of all persons.

VERBALIZATION VERSUS ACTION

For many years, it was assumed that significant changes in behavior could be brought about through verbalization alone, most change techniques centering about conversation between the change agent and his client. But of course these "conversations" were quite specialized and involved far more than those of everyday life.

We have recently witnessed a reemphasis upon nonverbal means of inducing and maintaining individual behavior change. Learning theory techniques, for example, often involve little or no significant verbal interchange between the change agent and the client. In the gestalt encounter group, persons are encouraged to *experiment* with different forms of behavior, to carry out actions that they might normally not undertake with others—and to learn from them. Various techniques derived from role theory require the person undergoing change to actually perform a series of behaviors. One such technique, *role pre-scription,* which we will discuss in detail later, involves a series of sessions in which the client constructs an ideal role for himself, tries it out in the real world outside of the change situation, revises it, tries the revision out, and so forth. It has become apparent that the way to change one's behavior is, in a very real sense, to *change one's behavior!* While this statement might, at first blush, seem paradoxical or even absurd, it is quite evident that verbal rehearsal of possible future actions is often insufficient. It is often the case that generalized changes in behavior can occur and be maintained only when the person is willing to begin trying such changes out under properly controlled conditions for action, feedback, and learning.

RESPONSIBILITY FOR CHANGE

Whether one person can actually change another is, of course, a matter of considerable controversy. Under conditions of complete control over another person, it is quite possible to induce behavioral changes, but aside from the extremely rare circumstances where such total control might obtain (e.g., the concentration camp), the change agent usually has a lesser degree of influence over his client and, in many situations, no control at all. It is therefore often the case that responsibility for change must rest with the client himself rather than with the change agent. That is, in the final analysis and for the most part, persons change themselves. This, of course, implies in no way that change agents do nothing in the change process. They may *facilitate* changes in their client in many ways. And it is here that differences among change theorists are noted. In some techniques, the change theorist himself may be quite active and, moreover, assume much of the responsibility for change in his client. This can be particularly true of individual change efforts based upon physical treatments where an expert applies surgical, chemical, or other forms of physical therapy to a relatively passive client. To some extent, it is also true of behavior control techniques where a trainer manipulates reward contingencies in order to produce the desired behaviors. On the other hand, change agent activity and responsibility can be virtually nonexistent in some approaches. Some techniques require full cooperation between an active agent and an equally active client. Others require a relatively passive agent and an extremely active and self-directed client. It is often the case, however, that persons seeking the services of change agents expect that things will be done to them and for them. In most techniques it is necessary that the client come to see that his role will require something of himself and, quite often, the client must discover the simple truth that change will not happen to him passively and miraculously; he himself must work to bring it about.

OUTCOMES OF A CHANGE PROCESS

An important but rarely discussed dimension of change efforts is the nature of the outputs of the process, or what the client learns as a consequence of participating in a program of change. At the simplest level, the learning may be quite specific and confined entirely to a change in behavior. The person may come to behave in a different way or he may acquire new perceptions of himself. This is, of course, a successful outcome and one whose importance cannot be minimized. However, an ideal change process should also give the person a sense of the process itself and leave him with an understanding of the means through which he can continuously monitor and change his behavior in social situations outside of the formal change situation. The analogy to the academic learning situation is quite clear. One can teach such that the students "know the material." Or one can teach such that they not only know the material but know why it is that they know it and, moreover, can begin to generate new knowledge on their own. In short, one must teach facts but, ideally, one must also teach how facts come to be facts and also how new facts can be discovered. The difference is one of teaching students to *memorize* and teaching students to *think*.

Similarly, in the self-learning that characterizes the individual change process, the person should ideally come to know something about the ways in which "facts" about himself and others come into being. He could also profit by knowing some of the *strategies* by which such learnings can be extended into new situations and throughout his life (Sechrest and Wallace, 1967; Wallace, 1971). One can readily see that this dimension touches on the question of whether or not the change process should be seen as being *fixed in time* or as a *continuous process,* one with temporary periods of stability, during which new forms of thought and behavior are consolidated, followed by further efforts.

THE ASSESSMENT OF OUTCOMES

The final dimension we shall consider is that of the assessment of outcomes. It is only within relatively recent times that serious efforts have been undertaken to evaluate the effectiveness of change efforts and the detailed and systematic analysis of outcomes is now only in its beginning stages. It is sad but true that the history of change technology has followed the familiar pattern of enthusiastic endorsement by the partisans of this or that approach with little empirical support for the often far-reaching and sometimes downright extravagant claims of effectiveness. Fads, cults, and true believers have been far too evident while the attitudes of caution, skepticism, and evaluative analysis have lagged very much behind. The reasons for this situation are fairly clear. First, it is often difficult to achieve reliable outcome data on individual change programs. Secondly, this area of investigation has tended to draw its practitioners from the ranks of the applied scientists rather than from those of the research minded methodologists. Finally, many change theories themselves are couched in such general and often ambiguous terms that it is impossible to generate clear operational statements of outcome criteria. Change theories have often seemed more literary in nature than scientific and while the more popular of them have attracted numerous advocates, both lay and professional, it is often the case that even these enthusiastic proponents cannot provide clear and unequivocal statements of what the change process is to accomplish, how it accomplishes what it does, and how one knows that it has accomplished what it purports to accomplish.

While new change techniques continue to appear with little or no data bearing upon their effectiveness, the situation does show definite signs of improvement. Practitioners of behavioral science can now be found who are equally at home in the research laboratory and the applied situation. Research methodologies for evaluating the difficult problem of assessing outcomes are steadily improving in precision and sophistication. And, perhaps of greatest importance, change agents of all kinds are increasingly recognizing that outcome research is a vital and necessary part of any change process. Nonetheless, the sophisticated *consumer* of such services must be reasonably cautious and skeptical when confronted with change agents whose evidence for the efficacy of their techniques consists largely of enthusiastic testimonials.

REQUIREMENTS FOR AN
ORGANIZATIONALLY RELEVANT THEORY

As we have seen, theories of individual change vary along a number of dimensions. In approaching a topic as complex as that of behavioral change, a dimensional analysis such as the one we have presented is useful precisely because it alerts us to the fact that *choices* are available. Moreover, when our efforts are directed toward understanding planned change of individual behavior in the context of the modern organization, it seems quite clear that the available theories of individual change are not all equally useful. In fact, choice among competing conceptualizations is essential.

What are the requirements for an *organizationally relevant theory of individual behavior change?* Let's consider this question in the light of our dimensions of analysis.

Individual versus socially oriented conceptions

From our perspective, a useful theory of individual change in the context of the organization should focus upon social factors in both the initiation and the maintenance of change. Aside from the impracticalities of the therapeutic, doctor-patient change relationship (e.g., formidable costs, the length of the process, lack of trained personnel in sufficient numbers, etc.), there are good theoretical reasons for such a choice. Organizational problems are rarely, if ever, problems of isolated actors. Most typically, the difficulties flow from the interactive behavior of one individual with another, from the relationships among individuals within a group of persons, and from the relationships between and among groups of individuals within the organization. Consequently, in order for a change effort to be successful it is necessary to draw as many of the concerned persons into the process as possible. When, for example, it is necessary for two persons within the organization to change their behavior vis-à-vis one another, the unit of analysis should be that particular interactive relationship. When two groups of persons interact with each other in a dysfunctional manner, the unit of analysis should be that of intergroup patterns of behavior. While it is certainly possible to find numerous instances where dramatic changes of behavior in a single individual may bring about desirable organizational outcomes, it is more often true that such changes in an individual are difficult to bring about in isolation from those significant others with whom he has important interactions. Such changes are exceedingly difficult to maintain, and, even if successful, paradoxically dysfunctional. One must remember that the organization is a system of dynamic *social* relationships. As with all complex systems, changing one element without changing others may actually be dysfunctional, if not impossible.

Minimal change versus maximal change

Theories of individual behavior change which assume that any change in overt behavior, no matter how trivial, must involve serious effort after total personality change seem of limited value in the organizational context. It is questionable to assume that *all* of a person's behavior is dynamically linked to underlying motives, needs, defenses, and conflicts, the majority of which are unconscious. In point of fact, it is probably of greater utility for one to assume that *none* of the overt behavior of individual actors is linked dynamically to hypothetical underlying forces. Such an assumption would permit one to experiment directly and straightforwardly with changes in a wide variety of organizationally relevant behaviors. It seems wise to keep one's assumptions about the determinants of behavior as simple as possible from the outset. If, after serious and persistent effort, change does not occur or is not maintained, then it may seem reasonable to broaden one's assumptions and search for more complex determinants of overt behavior. Some of these determinants may lie within the actor himself but others will surely lie external to the actor. In any case, lacking substantial empirical data one way or the other, it seems foolish to initiate a change effort employing the most complex set of assumptions that one can imagine. Experiment, feedback, and action in the real world of organizational behavior, rather than complex assumptions about the determinants of overt behavior should guide our actions.

Historical reconstructive approaches versus contemporary analysis

While considerable evidence testifying to the importance of early experience exists from animal studies, the data from longitudinal studies of human beings are equivocal. In point of fact, the picture of human personality development is more *inconsistent* than one would expect if early experience were really the prepotent determinant of adult behavior. Long-term studies of human personalities indicate that it is difficult to predict adult characteristics from measurements of childhood characteristics, equally difficult to predict adult characteristics from adolescent characteristics, and surprisingly difficult to predict adolescent characteristics from childhood ones (Kagan and Moss, 1962; Tuddenham, 1959; Rohrer and Edmonson, 1960). Despite both lay and professional belief in the significance of early experience, data clearly establishing the importance of such experience in human beings are strangely lacking. We do not, of course, mean to imply that traumas of an *extreme* nature have no influence over subsequent development, for such things as severe nutritional inadequacies in infancy, exceedingly harsh and brutal parental treatment of children, and violent tragedies can clearly continue to affect the lives of individuals as they mature and develop. For the most part, though, within the "normal" range of human developmental experiences, there seems to be no compelling reason for assuming that events *distant* in time are more powerful determinants of present behavior than relatively recent or contemporary events. Even the most casual examination of the lives of persons reveals that much of their present behavior is determined by their present life circumstances and, in numerous instances, their perceptions and elaborations of possible *futures*.

Aside from the question of the determinants of present behavior, one must also examine the assumption that present behavior cannot be *changed* without altering perceptions of past events, reliving past events, or recapturing the emotionality associated with past events. Experience with several change techniques (e.g., the sensitivity training laboratory and the encounter group) suggests quite strongly that substantial changes in present behavior can be brought about by an emphasis upon *present* behavior. Actually, experience with such techniques suggests that obsessive concern with past events may be one way that persons prevent themselves from changing present patterns of behavior. One's biography may provide one with a ready and convenient excuse for refusing to take any responsibility for present behavior, for the past is rich with persons whom we perceive as villainous and can and do blame for our present inadequacies. Moreover, it seems often the case that difficulties in such relationships as the intimate marital relationship or the superior-subordinate relationship seem magnified and exacerbated when the focus is upon the history of the relationship rather than upon the present circumstances. It is difficult enough to solve present problems without the intolerable stress of simultaneously attempting to deal with conflicting perceptions of past events, reawakened resentments, and imagined injustices.

In any event, it seems to us that the events of greatest concern to the individuals who make up a functioning organization are those that concern the present and those that lie in the reasonably forseeable future. The behavior of greatest importance to the change agent in the organization must be that which is directed toward these present and future events.

Structured versus unstructured change settings

The arguments which often arise in educational and training circles concerning the optimal degree of structure for learning seem to us to be largely misdirected. The central issue seems to be not whether such situations should be, in a general sense, structured or unstructured, but rather the *degree* of structure for the kind of learning and problem at hand. There are, for example, those sensitivity laboratory trainers who see the unstructured situation of the T-group as the only feasible situation for self-relevant learning and personal change. While it is certainly true that the unstructured T-group situation is ideal for certain kinds of learning and for facilitating certain changes, it is equally true that it cannot be generalized for all learning and to all settings in which change is required. It would appear that an ideal theory of organizational change would incorporate learning situations and techniques which vary in structure to suit the purpose at hand. It is certainly of value for organizational members to learn to cope with an unstructured situation and the problems arising therefrom, but it seems evident that organizational change will often involve more than that. Competence in situations of varying structure is more likely to be a requirement of organizational life than expertise in extreme situations only. More than one enthusiastic "graduate" of a weekend sensitivity training experience for executives has attempted to generalize the unstructured laboratory situation to the organizational setting indiscriminately and with dismaying results.

Feelings versus intellect

Within recent years, in a variety of change techniques, we have seen an extensive belief in the value of emotional catharsis. The assumption is frequently made that change is an emotional process and little else. Precisely why such *exclusive* focusing upon emotional release has recently preoccupied so many change agents is puzzling, for it has long been recognized in therapeutic situations that mere catharsis is not enough to induce lasting behavior change. While it is clear that people can be "turned on" in the context of the weekend training or encounter group where little beyond emotional release is accomplished, we have observed that being "turned on" doesn't last. Moreover, feelings of euphoria not only fail to be maintained outside the training experience, but we have also observed, in some cases, severe confusions and nontrivial depressions. We do not mean to imply that these are necessary outcomes of *any* training or encounter experience, but we certainly do wish to raise questions concerning the conduct of such groups and the ways in which such experiences can be structured.

The change process is one which involves both feelings and intellect. Neither can be safely ignored if significant and stable changes are to be expected. Above all, a person completing a change experience should be in a position to see quite clearly what he has *learned* as a consequence of participation. This learning will surely involve feelings, but it will also concern such things as his typical patterns of coping, his beliefs about himself and others, his expectations, hypotheses about situations in which he finds himself, and the alternative ways of thinking and behaving that are available to him.

Verbalization versus action

A change theory relevant to organizations must necessarily include action stages as well as those concerning preparation for action. Change techniques have too often focused upon verbal rehearsal and neglected the importance of planned action steps. Under these circumstances, verbalization often becomes a substitute for action. It is clearly time to question the assumption that change will automatically flow from the verbal analysis and rehearsal stage into the everyday activities of the person. The model should more appropriately be that of analysis and planning, action, feedback, further analysis and planning, action, feedback, and so on. In our opinion, one should assume very little about the impact of a change process on the real-life situation of the person in the organization. Action and feedback are integral parts of the process.

Responsibility for change

An effective organization is one in which individual members are capable of initiating necessary actions and assuming responsibility for their actions. The need to blame others for either personal or organizational shortcomings, like the tendency to locate the source of all one's miseries *outside* of oneself, is largely absent. In short, an effective organization is one in which members "own" their feelings and actions. We do not mean to minimize the many social influences apparent in the modern organization nor do we wish to devalue the importance of collaborative interdependent effort, but we do wish to emphasize that the individual need not be a blind and unwilling "victim" of the behavior of others. Effective interdependent effort is best accomplished by capable, responsible, and self-governing persons who have *chosen* to collaborate with others in the interests of task accomplishment.

The goals and techniques of organizational change programs should encourage or at least be consistent with the values of self-governance, individual responsibility, and mature interdependence. Change theories which minimize individual responsibility for change and encourage continued dependence upon a change agent therefore seem of questionable value in the organizational context.

Outcomes and assessment of outcomes

Much of what we have said in our earlier discussion of these dimensions reflects our beliefs here. An effective organizational change program is one which not only facilitates specific changes in behavior but imparts a sense of the process as well. It is our firm belief that no organizational change programs should be undertaken without including assessment procedures as an integral part of the process itself.

SUMMARY

In this chapter we have examined the dimensions along which theories of individual change vary. As we have seen, an analysis of this nature is valuable in exposing the *choices* available to us in understanding planned change within the context of the modern organization. We have utilized these choices in attempting to state the requirements of a theory of individual change relevant to the organizational context.

While the dimensional analysis should prove of some assistance in organizing and conceptualizing the considerable literature on individual change, it is perhaps most important as an aid to the reader in making explicit his own unexamined assumptions about change and how it is accomplished. Each of us, whether we have made a formal study or not, appears to have a "theory" about how to change the behavior of ourselves and others, and we often act on the bases of these unexamined and implicit "naive" theories. In a very real sense the management-administrative role is precisely that of a change agent. Managers are involved with human systems—systems that are dynamic, constantly in flux, phantasmagoric. In the face of such naturally occurring change, *planned and deliberate change* assumes major significance in the activities of the manager. And, as we have seen, individual behavior change is a critically important part of any planned change effort.

REFERENCES

Bandura, A., and R. H. Walters. *Social Learning and Personality Development*. Holt, Rinehart & Winston, 1963.

Ellis, A. *Reason and Emotion in Psychotherapy*. Lyle Stuart, 1962.

Janov, A. *The Primal Scream*. Putnam, 1970.

Kagan, J., and H. A. Moss. *Birth to Maturity: A Study in Psychosocial Development*. Wiley, 1962.

Kahn, R. L., D. M. Wolfe, R. P. Quinn, and D. J. Snoek. *Organizational Stress: Studies in Role Conflict and Ambiguity*. Wiley, 1964.

Menninger, K. *Theory of Psychoanalytic Technique*. Basic Books, 1958.

Rohrer, J. H., and M. S. Edmonson. *The Eighth Generation*. Harper & Row, 1960.

Sechrest, L., and J. Wallace. *Psychology and Human Problems*. Merrill, 1967.

Tuddenham, R. D. "Constancy of personality ratings over two decades." *Genet. Psychol. Monogr.* 60 (1959).

Wallace, J. *Psychology: A Social Science*. W. B. Saunders, 1971.

Wolpe, J. *Psychotherapy by Reciprocal Inhibition*. Stanford University Press, 1958.

Data Collection and Action Research

3

The collection of information can be a significant and potent part of the change strategy in any organization. The process of data collection serves several important and useful functions:

1) Data collection, if performed carefully and insightfully, can reduce the degree to which change is haphazard and relatively unplanned by creating a realistic information base for organizational diagnosis. It often leads to an increased awareness of the areas in which organizational behavior could be fruitfully and effectively changed.

2) Out of what is termed *pluralistic ignorance*, people often assume that their observations of the way the organization is functioning are unique, even when in fact these observations may be widely shared by others. One way of overcoming this gap in knowledge is through data collection. Revealing these commonly held perceptions often provides an impetus toward organizational problem-solving. It may provide a focus around which organization members can come to understand how other people feel about their jobs and about the ways in which the organization is functioning. People may become able, perhaps for the first time, to share with each other their perceptions, feelings, ideas, and other information bearing on the organization's performance. Information obtained from one

person or from one group can be linked systematically to that from other individuals or groups, and hence may provide a much fuller understanding of the current status of the organization and the available avenues for potential change.

3) Data collection, as the initial step in a change effort, has the effect of involving people at many levels in the organization in the assessment and diagnostic activities which are traditionally the domain of top management and are often conducted in a cautious, semisecretive manner.

DATA FROM ORGANIZATIONAL WORK GROUPS

Some of the methods of data collection and feedback have long been used under the name of survey feedback (Tannenbaum, 1966), a technique intended to induce changes in the organization or at least provide a basis for planning change. The method must employ both data collection and feedback to be effective and is usually designed to ascertain the attitudes and perceptions of organization members. The structure for the survey can include such dimensions as work, superiors, subordinates, top management, peers, and other aspects of the work situation.

The data, summarized and interpreted from such various points of view as those of organizational effectiveness, employee morale, and customer relations, are then discussed in groups. The groups may be drawn from, or consist of, such organizational families as a superior and those who report directly to him or the managers at one particular level. Since an individual is frequently a member of several work families, multiple membership can be a crucial element in the exploration and interpretation of data. Managers, particularly, play a coordinative role or "linking" function between the groups in which they hold membership. The sharing and communication of information in this process is the initial step in planned change.

In discussions of data, groups can compare their perceptions with those of other groups or with those of the organization as a whole. For example, differences between supervisors and the working level may be an important basis for discussion. Specific dissatisfactions and differences can begin a process of detailed interpretation and diagnosis. The "closer to home" the discussion, the more likely there is to be action, and the more there will be action on relevant issues.

The survey feedback method is most useful as a way of establishing a climate in which difficult problem areas can be openly shared and discussed. The feedback process involved utilizes more of the potential creativity in the organization to resolve organizational and administrative problems. It is also a way of establishing communication networks among members who, under other conditions, would rarely meet for such discussions. Other uses of established feedback groups may also be explored by the organization's leadership. For example, such groups may be used as task forces on specific organizational problems.

In concept, the survey feedback method is a predecessor of action research. While the major components of survey feedback are data collection and feedback of results, action research spells out more clearly the necessary elements in initiating such a procedure and then deals with those steps beyond feedback which ensure planned change (Margulies and Raia, 1968).

THE CONCEPT OF ACTION RESEARCH

Action research was first conceptualized by Kurt Lewin. He was interested in social change and hence felt that the process of action, evaluation, and feedback was critical in determining the direction and intensity of social change efforts.

Research, as such, is not typically seen as related to learning. Indeed, research and learning are most often viewed as two separate processes, the research process—the methods of hypothesis formulation, data collection, and hypothesis testing—and the learning process—the methods of forming conclusions from the results of research and formulating plans and actions. Most would agree, however, that action research is the means by which the research process and the learning process can be integrated. Action research is aimed at generating data which, through learning, can guide and direct social change. The notions and characteristics of action research are therefore important in the context of directed and planned organizational change and are essential to the assessment and evaluation of change efforts.

For the manager interested in initiating change in his organization it may be helpful to identify those characteristics of action research which assist in the formulation and implementation of data gathering plans and change programs. The next sections outline those characteristics typical of action and those typical of research. Neither should be ignored.

Action research is action

The following four characteristics of action research contribute to the action-learning component of the process:

1) *Problem orientation.* Action research is designed to explore, clarify, and identify the factors contributing to a problem the organization is experiencing. Without understanding these factors organizational change efforts designed to eliminate dissatisfactions are likely to be unsuccessful. Action research is designed both to provide data which can contribute to the organization's ability to take action on those critical problems and to create a climate in which organizational learning can take place. The solution of problems is only one aim; solving problems so that they stay solved is another.

2) *Involvement of the client system.* Inherent in the action research approach is the immediate and direct involvement of the organization in the problem-solving process. Sometimes, with help from a consultant, the organization can participate in the formulation of hypotheses, in the design of data gathering methods, and in the implementation of those methods. Action research emphasizes the organization's responsibility for engaging in problem solving and for developing internal capabilities for dealing with its own critical issues instead of projecting that responsibility to external factors. In this way action research can provide permanent organizational learning rather than simple solutions to discrete problems.

3) *Problem-solving and data gathering as a continuous process.* Action research can become part of the organization's pattern for dealing with its own behavior. By learning to collect data and examine its processes continuously, the organization can make problem-solving and change a way of organizational life rather than a response to some crisis. One kind of important learning for the organization, then, is how to design and conduct, and evaluate the data from, action research, and to do so expediently and efficiently.

4) *Feedback of results.* Data collected by action research should be made available in as timely and efficient a manner as possible. The people in the organization who were respondents in "the research process," having supplied the data, now become recipients of it. In this way the information is used not simply for research purposes but is incorporated into the

learning process in the organization by providing a basis for examination and diagnosis of real and pressing issues. By carefully considering how data are to be assimilated and how they are to be channeled into action plans, changes within the organization have a high likelihood of being initiated and implemented. The research process itself may be monitored and guided by members of the organization in conjunction with experienced and skilled external people.

Action research is research

As much as action research contributes to organizational learning in an action-evaluation-action sense, action research is also very much research. Put quite simply, research is here the studious and scientific inquiry into the critical phenomena of organizational behavior. It is the study of those organizational factors which contribute to or detract from the achievement of the organization's stated goals. The research process is important in the formulation of a change program because it can either verify or disprove what people in the organization think they know about the organization and how it is functioning. It is also critical to establishing a realistic information base and formulating attainable change objectives. The following characteristics describe the research component of the action research process.

The development of models and hypotheses • Very often the action research method begins with the formulation of hypotheses derived from members of the organization about the interrelationships of certain organizational factors. A hypothesis is simply a tentative explanation for observed occurrences, an explanation which can be investigated systematically. The method may also begin with the development of models as useful tools for describing the processes and the ways in which the organization proceeds to accomplish its tasks. The relationships of the components or variables in the model can then often be stated as hypotheses to be tested by applying the research methodology.

Data gathering is hypothesis oriented • The specific data collected (and even the methods used) in an organization are implicitly, if not explicitly, guided by the initial perception of the organizational problems and by the kinds of information the organization is interested in. Hypotheses (those tentative explanations) are usually present even when they are difficult to state. It is advantageous for people in the organization to make those explanations as explicit as they can so that they can then systematically test their thinking, their assumptions, and their perceptions of how the organization functions.

The use of research results • In addition to providing the information upon which the organization can base its action plans, research results may indeed add to what we know about organizations and organizational behavior. Research results, therefore, should be viewed in the broader context of theory and practice in administration. Although each organization and suborganization is indeed unique, these systems also exhibit characteristics which are at least somewhat similar to other organizations. Every time research is done in an organization it either modifies, negates, or supports what we think we know about organizational behavior. The effective manager sees himself as part of a stream of experience in administrative and organizational technology, and, as such, views his organization (or subunit) in the broader context in which it is embedded.

The two objectives of action research (action planning and learning by research) are very often perceived as being in conflict. On the one hand, the members of the organization are likely to perceive the sole objective of action research as the formulation of action plans and directions for change in the organization, while on the other the external action researcher views the information as part of the store of knowledge in the area of organizational behavior. The two are not incompatible and both objectives may be achieved when both are taken into consideration in the design and implementation of action research plans (Lippitt, 1961; Bradford, Gibb, and Benne, 1964). It is possible to bring this about when the organization exhibits a willingness to participate in a process of scientific inquiry and experimentation and when the external action researcher remains aware that the problem situation requires concrete action decisions. In this framework research and problem-solving are done in an integrative manner and as part of the system of learning required by the organization to achieve significant changes in its character, its structure, and its behavior.

METHODS OF DATA GATHERING

There are many methods available for collecting data in and about an organization and the selection of one such method is of strategic importance. The most critical criterion of choice is applicability to the problem and to the organizational setting, though often choices on this basis are easier to recommend than to do. Judgment and experience are perhaps the best guidelines to selection. The success of a method can only be evaluated by its success in yielding adequate, reliable information which is useful from both objectives of action research. Although data gathering methods are described below, the reader should keep clearly in mind the context in which such methods are presented. The haphazard and mechanical application of technique is likely to yield disappointing results and to obstruct rather than facilitate planned change. The action research approach to data collection, although not necessarily as rigorous as other more academically conceived methods, can nevertheless have a significant impact on organizational change.

The survey questionnaire

One very quick way of obtaining information is the survey questionnaire. In this method questions are designed to get at specific kinds of information. Questionnaires are then constructed and distributed to informants, usually, but not necessarily, organization members. The questions themselves can be very specific and structured and require simply a checked response. Such responses lend themselves readily to quantitative analysis, but if the questionnaire is not thoughtfully designed, the results may prove of limited use. Hence pretesting questionnaires of this type may provide important insurance against useless expenditure of time and energy.

Sometimes questions can be more open-ended in nature, and allow the respondent to express his feelings and opinions on the subject freely. In this case the analysis of responses must be done by the "researcher" and a wider variation in perspectives can then be obtained. To be sure, analysis of this kind is more difficult, more costly, and more time consuming, but it can prove much more informative and useful.

In addition, a variety of existing questionnaires have reasonable validity and can be used. One such instrument is the system developed by Likert in which organizational behavior has been precoded into seven major variables: character of motivational forces, communication processes, interactional processes, decision-making processes, goal-setting processes, control processes, and performance characteristics (Likert, 1967). The organization may choose to elaborate several of these variables and ignore others depending on what it believes to be critical informational areas. For the most part, however, such instruments only provide a start at data collection.

The most useful questionnaires, from an action research point of view, are those developed by the manager and a representative sample of the population he wishes to canvass (Fordyce and Weil, 1971, p. 138).

The interview method

The interview method provides an opportunity to get information first hand from the respondent in a face-to-face situation. In this case key people, or a good sampling of people in the organization, may be interviewed at length about items of particular pertinence to organizational function. Like questionnaires, interviews may be very specific and require detailed information about certain areas (the structured interview) or they may be rather open-ended, and allow the respondent to express freely whatever seems pertinent or whatever has high priority for him at the moment (the unstructured interview). The key, in either the structured or unstructured mode, is that the respondent needs some guidance to what is expected of him. Successful interviews require skilled interviewers and enough time so that the interview can be managed. It is important for the interviewer to create a rapport with the interviewee rather quickly and direct the interview into pertinent avenues. Both the questionnaire and the interview require planning, though the face-to-face situation permits more flexibility and deviation than is possible with the questionnaire method.

When the organization is considering the use of an external organizational consultant to facilitate the change process, interviews provide an opportunity for close contact between the consultant and organizational members. The rapport developed during the interviews may become important in later work.

Organizational sensing

Sensing is a relatively new data collection technique. Its major purpose is to obtain quickly both information on current feelings about how well the organization is functioning and a tentative identification of significant problem areas experienced by people in the organization. In essence, organizational sensing is akin to widespread generation and identification of the issues confronting the organization and affecting its effectiveness.

A sensing session takes the form of an unstructured group

interview. Such sessions can involve the manager so that he can obtain information directly from his subordinates, or from several levels below him in the organization, or they can involve an objective third party obtaining information from any or all groups within the organization. There are a variety of different formats which can be employed in a sensing session. These may vary both in the degree of structure and in the selection of participants. Sensing sessions, very much like questionnaires or interviews, should be well planned. Questions should be carefully designed, participants should be selected and sampled, and careful thought should be given to communicating the purpose of the session to its participants.

Sensing sessions are potential problem-solving sessions. The interaction of the group not only generates data but lets ideas and solutions to uncovered problems be explored as well. Cross sections of the organization can be employed to look at operations from the point of view of interdepartmental and overall organizational concerns while groups from the same subunit can bring things "closer to home." Although this method does not permit as rigorous an analysis as do interviews and questionnaires, it nevertheless is a useful means of opening channels of communication between levels and across horizontal groups in the organization.

Longitudinal methods

Another way of continuing to collect data in an organization is to create a climate in which pertinent data is kept and stored over time. For example, it may be advantageous for a manager or a team to keep records of critical incidents which can later be used as pertinent data. Other methods, such as managerial logs or the use of diaries, can also be useful for analyzing over time those things which crop up as organizational issues or problems, and also as a way of focusing more freely on the way in which the organization traditionally deals with particular kinds of problems.

Structured observational techniques

With a little practice managers can become skillful in the use of structured observational formats. In these methods behavior is categorized and analyzed so that a picture along the dimensions represented by the categories can be drawn. One common technique of this type is Benne and Sheats' (1948) Functional Role Analysis method. Theoretically, effective problem-solving groups exhibit behavior in two dimensions, those of *task* behavior and *group maintenance* behavior. Both are essential if the group is to be effective. Within these two major dimensions categories are created which classify behavior into the specific roles people assume in organizational problem-solving. With this kind of analysis the organization may come to understand better those roles which are predominant in its problem-solving style, and those roles which people may be encouraged to assume to enhance the organization's problem-solving effectiveness. Some groups may lack the kinds of skills represented by roles in either dimension. In this case, role training techniques such as those discussed in Chapter 3 can be utilized effectively.

One dimension lists *task* roles—these are the kinds of roles which focus on the specific behavior members of the group must exhibit to accomplish the task before them. Some of the roles in this category are:

Information giver—offers facts or generalizations which are authoritative or relates his own experience pertinent to the group problem.

Information seeker—asks for authoritative information and facts pertinent to the problem being discussed.

Opinion giver—states his belief or opinion about suggestions or alternative points of view.

Opinion seeker—asks less for the facts than for alternative suggestions or values which may pertain to the group undertaking.

Clarifier—shows or clarifies the relationships among various ideas and suggestions; tries to pull ideas and suggestions together.

Elaborator—spells out suggestions in terms of examples; tries to imagine and show how an idea or suggestion would work out if adopted by the group.

The second dimension lists *building and maintenance* roles, which are concerned with *facilitating* the problem-solving processes in the organization or group. These include such roles as:

Harmonizer—mediates the differences between other members and attempts to reconcile disagreements.

Encourager—praises, supports, and accepts the contributions of others; in various ways indicates understanding and acceptance of diverse points of view.

Gate keeper—attempts to keep communication channels open by encouraging or facilitating the participation of others.

Group observer—keeps records of various aspects of group process and feeds such data with proposed suggestions back into the group's evaluation of its progress.

Compromiser—attempts to resolve conflicts in ideas or positions by focusing on alternatives and other points of view.

Since the theoretical premise is that both *task* and *building and maintenance* roles are necessary for effective problem-solving, the organization may analyze the distribution of such role behaviors in its problem-solving process. It can then explicitly decide which roles need to be encouraged in order to enhance its problem-solving capability.

The organization mirror

The "organization mirror" is a way for an organizational unit to collect information from a number of other key organizational units to which it relates. In this case the relevant units reflect back to the receiving unit perceptions and information regarding its performance. The participating units act as a mirror to provide an often unavailable perspective for the organization receiving feedback. The mirror is also applicable to getting data from other organizations such as customers and suppliers.

This technique is particularly useful when an organization feels that relationships with other groups or organizations can be improved. The method simply allows the recipients to listen, categorize, and analyze firsthand reports about their performance. The most useful thing about the mirror is that it involves both the recipients of the data and the respondents in problem-solving to improve effectiveness. The information is not allowed to grow stale and out of date, but is used on the spot to generate changes.

An organizational consultant, skilled in the design of meetings, can employ a variety of techniques to generate and display the data. For example, in one design the respondents discuss among themselves how they see the particular organization functioning—in both the positive and the negative aspects of the operation. The recipients are asked to record the data and categorize them, but not to interject until the next step, which might include task groups of both recipients and respondents to identify the major problem areas, set priorities, and begin the development of solutions (Fordyce and Weil, 1971, pp. 101–105).

The organization mirror really epitomizes the action research concept. Very often organization mirror sessions evolve from data gathering meetings to problem-solving sessions in which the problem-solvers are those who have a vested interest in the solutions.

Self-generated scales

There are occasions where the dimensions of organizational life can best be determined by those directly concerned. It is often only the members of the group who can decide which factors are likely to have the greatest impact on its effectiveness. When these factors have been established and agreed upon they can be used as scale items for questionnaires or group sensing sessions as a way of generating group or organizational data in specified areas. This method can perhaps best be understood by way of an example.

There are occasions when work teams, management teams, or coordinating groups find it necessary to assess their performance. (The notion of teams and team development is discussed in Chapter 7.) The group may begin by listing those characteristics that it considers significant in an effectively functioning group performing its particular task (managing a school district or coordinating an engineering project, etc.). Groups normally find this rather easy to do and create lists of between 15 and 35 characteristics, some of which are common to most groups while others seem to depend on the particular function the group is performing.

In the next step each group member then rates the group on each of the generated characteristics. The rating scale consists of ten points, 10 meaning the greatest possible effectiveness and 1 the least. For example, the following table consists of a list of scales generated by a group together with the composite group rating for each scale.

An alternative is to plot each member's ratings of the group so that a quick look at the differences and similarities in perceptions of the group can also be obtained. In either case the group has available to it a picture of how its members assess its effectiveness. The next step involves a determination of where change is possible and how changes can be made to improve the group's functioning. For instance, the group

Characteristics of an Effective Group	Most Effective 10	9	8	7	6	5	4	Least Effective 3	2	1
1. Clearly defined goals	x									
2. Open communication							x			
3. Feelings openly expressed							x			
4. Information sharing						x				
5. Activities well planned						x				
6. Highly motivated members							x			
7. Conflicts openly resolved						x				
8. Minimal dysfunctional interperson hostility						x				
9. High participation						x				
10. High technical skills						x				
11. Availability of information							x			
12. Technical leadership	x									
13. Work of individuals well coordinated						x				

responsible for the above profile might elect to do something about (11), availability of information, or (6), the motivation of group members, or (9), the amount of participation.

This method, then, is not only a way of generating data for the group, but it provides a logical lead-in to action aimed at improving the quality of the group's function. The group can elect at a later date to make a similar set of judgments to see if any movement has taken place as a result of trying to improve one or more characteristics. In essence the group has created its own gauge, one which it can use over and over again in self-assessment.

This self-rating technique can also be used by any group that wishes to see itself as others see it (see also the discussion of the organizational mirror). It has the advantage of representing the group's own criteria for effectiveness and of being flexible enough to be tailored to the situation.

Another approach, applicable to work teams, is for each member to rate (from a high of 5 to a low of 1) every member (including himself) on relevant team behavior. For example, such dimensions as participation, contribution to joint goals, honesty with one another, etc., might be chosen. A matrix can be developed and posted which has the *raters* down the vertical axis and *being rated* across the horizontal axis.

		Being Rated				
		Joe	Bill	Bob	Tom	John
	Joe					
	Bill					
Raters	Bob					
	Tom					
	John					

Dimension: Contribution to team goals.

This procedure may provide a basis for discussion leading to improved team operation. Again, the team can decide to generate such data periodically as a way of monitoring their progress.

The method has the advantage of being a group product. Everyone participates in its development. It usually reaches the issues quickly and lets actions be developed in immediate response. It is perhaps used best by small teams which have had some history of working together. The only caution is that unless everyone agrees to participate in data collection the reliability of the data may be questionable.

Some factors in data gathering methods

The method of gathering data to bring about change can have direct impact on the success of the change effort. Data gathering methods can be placed somewhere on a continuum, the ends of which may be labeled to correspond to any of a variety of paired factors which contribute to the choice of a method. One such labeling, a common way of looking at data gathering methods, is to identify the continuum as one of *directness*. Survey questionnaires, for example, are less direct as a way of gathering information than sensing sessions. The following is a list of examples of the dimensions along which data gathering methods may be ranked:

A) Direct—Indirect
B) High problem-solving activity—Low problem-solving activity
C) Structured—Unstructured
D) Time consuming—Less time consuming
E) Easy to administer—Difficult to administer

Each data collection method then has its own profile or characteristic as described by these factors. It may even behoove an organization to create its own profile for the data gathering method it wishes to employ. The profile can then enable an organization to make ready decisions of which data gathering technique is most appropriate for its particular situation. The profile for each data gathering method can be compared with the profile as drawn up for the organizational situation. For example, the organization can make decisions about whether or not it wishes the data gathering method to include more or less problem-solving. It can make decisions about whether or not it wishes to engage in more direct or less direct methods of collecting information, or about how much time it is willing to devote to data gathering. Hence these decisions provide a basis for comparing the methods available and allow the one which matches the desired organizational profile to be selected.

Decisions are best made when these factors are considered in the light of the problem situation and the organizational climate. Some methods, to be successful, require a more open, trusting, collaborative climate than do others. To employ these methods in a climate which is suspicious, resistive, and competitive could not only lead to questionable results but could impair the changes being sought.

CASE ILLUSTRATION: DATA COLLECTION

The following case is intended to provide the reader with an opportunity to see how several data collection techniques were used in one organization. In addition, it is an illustration of the use of data collection as a means of initiating necessary organizational changes. The *Background* section is included to set the context for the data gathering plan described later and the organizational problems identified through the data gathering process. The factors contributing to the data collection methods used are highlighted.

Background

The organization of this case (for a detailed description of the case and the methods employed, see Margulies, 1972) is one of several departments in a large R&D organization. The department provides engineering support to a variety of aerospace systems designed by this firm. It employs about 200 people, of which about 50 are engineers and about 100 are engineering technicians, while the remainder are administrators, clerks, and technical data support people. Although the department has been reasonably stable in terms of its current size, its responsibilities have been increasing. Forecasts of its role indicate that the department is likely to become more and more responsible for key developmental functions of the parent organization.

The operating style which evolved in the early stages of this organization contributed strongly to its success. In the formative periods unilateral decision-making and isolation of effort were feasible, practical, and, in most instances, very necessary. Though useful in some ways, these factors fostered conditions where cross-communication was at a minimum and exchange of information was limited. Key members of the organization developed a parochial attitude and style in their actions and relations with each other. Activities were clearly delineated and separated, and ownership of those activities held high importance.

In an effort to ensure the effectiveness of the department in the light of its new responsibilities, management decided to initiate the changes necessary for resolving the operating difficulties. Top management and representatives from middle management, with some expert assistance, decided that a data collection and feedback process would be an appropriate and necessary first step. Management felt that it was important to involve people in thinking about the organization and about ways in which things could be improved. Morale appeared to be low but most of the management people involved in early planning seemed to feel that people really "had a lot to say," and would be willing to contribute to organizational improvement.

Although some organizational problems seemed fairly evident, the decision to engage in widespread data collection in the organization was based on several factors. First, management was interested in getting the benefit of many perspectives on the organization and how it was operating. Second, they felt that changes could be more easily implemented and supported when as many people as possible could be involved in planning the changes. Third, they felt the data collection process would also serve as a vehicle for people to begin discussions about the organization that would normally not take place. These factors, arrived at from a managerial perspective, parallel the general functions of data gathering as an initial step in a change effort.

A planning group consisting of representatives from all organizational levels and all functional areas was established. This group, with some outside help from people trained in data gathering methods, had the responsibility for the design and implementation of a data gathering plan. The question before the planning group was: What guidelines can we adopt to help in the preparation of our plan? The following seemed appropriate to the situation:

> A) The more direct the method of data gathering, the better. Firsthand information was deemed most desirable and any method should accommodate this notion.
>
> B) The plan should permit the involvement of as many people as possible in problem identification.
>
> C) The plan should be designed to elicit specific information.
>
> D) Since time was not a critical factor, the plan should provide management personnel an opportunity for an in-depth exploration of organizational functioning and should elicit a reasonably detailed diagnosis of organizational problems from each manager.

The resulting plan was built around two *interdependent* phases. The *first phase* was a number of *sensing sessions* with employees at the working level. The *second phase* involved in-depth interviews with all management personnel.

In *phase one* a sampling of 20 percent of the employees was chosen and groups of five people were formed. The groups met for approximately an hour to discuss several general themes. These themes included such things as:

> 1) What kinds of things, as you see them, contribute most to your job effectiveness?

2) What kinds of things contribute least to (or impede) your job effectiveness?

3) What kinds of things would you most like to change in the way the organization functions?

4) In your opinion, what should concern management most about the way the organization now functions?

5) What are your expectations for the future of this organization?

These questions were simply listed so that the group could proceed to discuss any of them in whatever order seemed most appropriate to them. Several training staff people participated as recorders. Each group was instructed to discuss the questions and to try to provide an arena in which information, feelings, and perceptions could be expressed. These *sensing* sessions were designed so that membership in sensing groups came from the same suborganization so that there could be some focus on problems of the subunit in which sensing session members worked, as well as on total department issues.

After all the phase one sensing sessions were held, members of the training staff who had recorded the discussions met with the planning group. Again, with some expert assistance, the data were first categorized according to each question and an analysis performed to ascertain the major problem areas pinpointed by the discussions. The following list represents a sample of some of the problem areas:

1) Prevailing vagueness about the objectives, goals, and directions toward which the department was working.

2) Behavior of the top management teams appeared to be uncoordinated and fraught with unresolved conflicts.

3) Communication in a timely and efficient manner seemed to need improvement.

4) Coordination and cooperation among functional units was difficult because of a lack of understanding of the contribution of each functional area to the accomplishment of the department mission.

5) Absence of ongoing assessment of training needs and provisions for meeting those needs. Although keeping up with new developments was critical, it was not happening in any concerted way in the department.

6) Interdivisional relationships were tense and stressful; rivalry and mistrust seemed to prevail.

The issues derived from the sensing sessions provided a basis for structuring the interviews in phase two.

Phase two of the data gathering plan called for interviews with management. The questions for these interviews were derived in part from the issues identified in phase one, with those items which seemed to deserve further exploration being included in the interview. For example, since the top team's behavior and interdivisional relationships seemed to be important issues, each manager interviewed was asked to explore these areas. Other questions were more general and asked for a broader perspective. Some of the questions used in the interview are presented below.

Management interview question schedule

1) "As you think about your job and your division, what things impinge upon your doing the most effective job you can"?

2) "What things, as you see it, really facilitate your getting your job done"?

3) "As you think about yourself and your job, what 'binds' or conflicts do you most often find yourself in"?

4) "How effectively do you see the department head and division heads functioning in their roles"?

5) "How would you describe the top team functioning"?

6) "How would you see the management team in your division operating"?

7) "How would you describe relationships with other divisions"?

8) "In what specific ways is it necessary for the divisions to work together"?

9) "How would other divisions describe relations with your division"?

10) "What would you think are major concerns of people with regard to training and career development"?

11) "How would you summarize the major concerns of people below your level"?

12) "If you had to summarize, what issues, if resolved, would improve the overall effectiveness of the department"?

Later, the interviewers met with the planning group. Information was summarized by question, and major departmental and divisional problem areas were identified. Relationships were drawn between issues derived from the sensing sessions and those derived from the interviews. It appeared that there was a good deal of agreement among all levels in the organization as to the problems this organization needed to attack if its efficiency were to be improved. Below are some of the issues derived from the interviews.

Summary of issues from phase two management interviews

1) Need for a clearer picture of the goals and directions of the department was evident.

2) Need to keep current on "what's happening"—communication and keeping informed in a timely manner was a major problem.

3) Lack of understanding of relevant functions and organizational relationships in the department was causing undue relational tension.

4) Training and career development was a top priority issue; there was need for developing a method for ongoing assessment of training needs.

5) Lack of top management coordination—too much energy was being wasted.

6) Relationships between groups that must work together were poor. Divisional working relationships needed to be improved.

Feedback and action planning

Once the information from both the *phase one sensing* sessions and *phase two interviewing* had been synthesized, a number of feedback sessions were conducted. The data were presented to work groups in the form of an *inventory of strengths and problems confronting the department*. Discussions about the data then proceeded in small groups (4–5 persons). The objective was to identify those issues which people felt held high priorities. Once the priorities were determined, the groups proceeded to work on setting up mechanisms to deal with the major issues. The first feedback session was conducted with the total group of department managers. Subsequent feedback sessions of the same kind were held at the divisional level as well. The data pertinent to each division were used in these sessions.

What began as a data gathering plan concluded in problem-solving activities in many areas in this department. The data gathering procedures grew out of an action research framework in which the organization itself participated in the design of the plan and produced, as well as received, the data.

The action research model is one in which research data is used as learning material to provide a basis for change. In this case the organization was able to transform the data available to it into action plans designed to resolve its major problems.

SUMMARY

In this chapter several things were discussed. Of major importance is the notion of action research. Action research is characterized by a data-action-evaluation process that inheres in most successful change attempts. This concept will appear again in discussions of the use of role-playing techniques, team development, and laboratory method.

A variety of techniques were described which the manager can employ to generate data in his organization. These techniques include some of the more common methods such as the interview and the questionnaire, as well as such variations of these basic tools as sensing sessions, the organizational mirror, and self-generated scales.

The important thing to remember is that any technique, no matter how simple or sophisticated, is not meant to be used haphazardly. The manager must weigh carefully the time, cost, level of participation, and the amount of structure required to do the job, all of which dramatically influence the appropriateness of one technique over another. The spirit of action research and the commitment to using the data in the service of improving the qualities of organizational life and output are underlying guidelines.

REFERENCES

Benne, K. D., and P. Sheats. "Functional roles of group members." *Journal of Social Issues,* 4 (Spring 1948): 42–47.
Bradford, L. P., J. R. Gibb, and K. D. Benne, eds. *The Laboratory*

Method in T-Group Theory and Laboratory Method, pp. 32, 33. Wiley, 1964.

Fordyce, J. K., and R. Weil. *Managing With People,* Addison-Wesley, 1971.

Likert, R. *The Human Organization.* McGraw-Hill, 1967.

Lippitt, R. "Value-judgement problems of the social scientist in action-research." In *The Planning of Change.* W. G. Bennis, K. D. Benne, and R. Chin, eds., pp. 689–94. Holt, Rinehart & Winston, 1961.

Margulies, N. "Coping with organizational change." *Synopsis* (January-February 1972).

Margulies, N., and A. P. Raia. "Action research and the consultative process." *Business Perspectives* (Fall 1968).

Tannenbaum, Arnold S. *Social Psychology of the Work Organization,* pp. 114–16. Wadsworth, 1966.

Learning and Change

4

All organizations can be viewed as *social learning systems.* Common processes and structures ensure that certain patterns of behavior will be acquired, other patterns maintained and reliably performed, and still other patterns of behavior eliminated or avoided in the organizational context. While much of this learning is deliberate, explicit, and formally sanctioned, much learning of significance is incidental, implicit, and not formally sanctioned. It is now well recognized that contradictory learning systems can exist within the same organization. Learned patterns of behavior which are functional for the individual or for some group of individuals are often totally incompatible with the achievement of overall organizational goals and objectives. Paradoxically, it is often the behavior of management itself that *directly* encourages the development of contradictory social learning systems. Moreover, management may *indirectly* contribute by failing to understand the organization as a human social learning system and consequently failing to act to produce a system that brings individual, group, and organizational learning into congruence.

In his role as change agent, the manager should take advantage of the powerful social learning factors that exist in all organizations. At the very least, he should have some understanding of how the organization as a social learning system operates. In this chapter, we will examine some important features of such a system.

ORGANIZATIONAL CULTURES

Although numerous definitions of the concept exist, we shall use the term "culture" to refer to the learned beliefs, values, and characteristic patterns of behavior that exist within an organization. One must not suppose that all organizations exhibit a single uniform and homogeneous system of learned beliefs, values, and patterns of behavior. Although some organizations may approach such cultural uniformity, variation is more characteristic. In some organizations, one can identify at least two cultural systems, formal and informal. The formal culture may consist of idealized statements of what the values, beliefs, and behaviors of members *should* be. The informal culture may consist of these as they *really are*. All organizations show this dichotomy, though in some one may be able to identify several informal cultures.

It is frequently the case that conflicts among and between the beliefs, values, and behavior patterns of the various cultures within the organization not only prevent the accomplishment of organizational goals but serve to maintain the status quo by hampering and, in some cases, actually sabotaging organizational change efforts. Change agents who attempt change programs in ignorance of the cultural context of the organization may thus find their time and effort wasted.

CONDITIONS THAT ENCOURAGE MULTIPLE CULTURES WITHIN THE ORGANIZATION

Several factors, if present, are indicative of multiple and conflicting cultures within an organization. First, organizations that draw their personnel from two or more significantly different populations are likely to have different cultural systems. This is especially true if members remain differentiated after organizational membership is achieved. For example, organizations that contain both military and civilian personnel may exhibit problems associated with these two different cultural systems. Class, ethnic, and racial differences may also contribute, particularly if such differences are emphasized within the organizational context by such conditions as work assignment or physical location.

Second, diverse organizational cultures may develop naturally around task related matters. Production workers may come to possess beliefs, values, and behaviors very different from those of research and development personnel. These may, in part, be a logical outcome of the requirements of different tasks (Lawrence and Lorsch, 1967).

Third, the organization's systems of rewards may unwittingly foster patterns of behavior, beliefs, and values in a particular subculture which are at variance with those of the total organization's stated goals as well as the goals of other subcultures within the organization. For example, Ullman (1967) has shown that in the psychiatric hospital, when total institutional funding depends on the number of patients cared for at a given time, staff behaviors are directed more toward maintaining a high patient population than toward curing and discharging patients. These individual behaviors obviously conflict with the formal treatment goals of the organization.

A final factor likely to evoke distinct subcultures within the organization is that of significant cultural change in the external society. In the past decade, we have witnessed within American society rapid and important changes. That such external cultural changes should begin appearing in the organizational context is not surprising. In all cultures in transition, "old" beliefs and values can sharply conflict with "new" ones. And as we have seen in recent events, the emerging values of authenticity, emotional expressiveness, trust, willingness to risk, collaboration, and individuality can conflict sharply with previously held values of "gamesmanship," emotional concealment, distrust, caution, competition, and conformity (Schmidt, 1970).

We by no means wish to leave the impression that cultural diversity within the organization is of necessity an undesirable condition, for it can certainly serve to stimulate healthy disagreement. Our point is simply that the manager, in his role as change agent, should be constantly aware of the possible existence of systematic differences in beliefs, values, and patterns of behavior within his organization. He should also be able to recognize when such diversity is related to dysfunctional organizational behavior and must, of course, be dealt with.

SOCIALIZATION: THE TRANSMISSION OF ORGANIZATIONAL CULTURE

It is now generally recognized that cultures are transmitted to new members through *socialization* processes. There now exists a considerable body of evidence that changes occur in individuals as a consequence of organizational membership. The new member is said to have undergone a process of organizational socialization as he moves from the status of "new member" to "old-timer" in the course of his organizational career. What are the essential ingredients of the socialization process? We shall discuss three: reinforcement, social modeling, and direct instruction.

Reinforcement

A large body of psychological literature exists to show that the behavior of organisms of all kinds, including human beings, can be influenced significantly by proper conditions of reinforcement. At the simplest level, we can think of reinforcement in terms of the consequences or outcomes of any given behavior. Behaviors that lead to valued outcomes are likely to be retained by the individual and reliably performed whereas behaviors that do not are likely to be abandoned. The simplicity of this central idea may easily lead one to ignore the importance of reinforcement in the complexities of everyday life, but even the most casual reading of the psychological literature will convince one that a complete understanding of social systems and the manner in which they can be changed requires a clear recognition of the importance of reinforcement. While it is obvious that many factors other than reinforcement influence behavior, the effects of rewards and punishments on our behaviors are much too important to ignore with impunity.

Individual differences in reinforcers

One must not suppose that all events are equally reinforcing for all individuals. As with human behavior generally, wide individual differences are apparent. For some persons, money may be a highly desired outcome. For others, social factors such as recognition, praise, and acceptance may be far more important than material things. These individual differences in reinforcers must be borne in mind when considering the applications of reinforcement theory to organizational change. We will have more to say on this point in our discussion of techniques of change derived from social learning theory.

Unwitting reinforcement

It is often the case that dysfunctional organizational behaviors occur because of unwitting or unintended reinforcement. Managers who take the time to investigate may discover that many problematic organizational behaviors are present precisely because they are reinforced by managerial behaviors. It is often the case that entire *organizational reward structures* are such that they mitigate against the achievement of organizational goals. The modern American university, for example, created many of its own problems by permitting an organizational reward structure that discouraged professors from interacting with students or involving themselves seriously in the activities necessary for the maintenance and continued survival of the organization. As a consequence, many professors correctly perceived that their immediate best interests were served by such things as "grantsmanship," frequent although premature and even trivial publication, and total involvement with their own scholarly activities to the neglect of students and the organization as a whole.

It is now well recognized that managers may contribute to the development of subordinate duplicity bordering on downright lying and cheating by managerial practices that reinforce secrecy, deception, and mistrust. In many organizations, workers forced to choose between leaving a record of work that looks good up top rather than doing those jobs that need to be done in the interests of the organization, are likely to choose the former. And it is often the case that false and misleading information continues to flow from lower levels of the organization to upper levels precisely because of managerial practices that reinforce and hence maintain such undesirable subordinate behaviors.

Reinforcement schedules

Reinforcements can be made available on a variety of differing schedules. They can be made to occur following every performance of a desired behavior or spread intermittently, administered as a fixed or variable number of reinforcements during a given time period. Since it has been shown that the manner in which reinforcements are scheduled can have important effects on behavior, it is curious that so little work has been done upon organizational reward structures and the scheduling of reinforcements. In any given organization, it might very well be that the desirable changes in behavior that might accompany a shortening or lengthening of the interval between pay days would be worth the costs incurred.

As with other individual differences, persons show differences in response to the scheduling of reinforcements. Some persons can continue to perform effortful responses for long periods of time before receiving their reinforcements. Others seem to require much more frequent reinforcement to maintain their interest and performance. A knowledge of these idiosyncratic differences is of considerable value in designing organizational change programs based upon reinforcement theory.

Intrinsic reinforcement
and self-administered rewards

The applications of reinforcement theory do not necessarily require an external agent to administer the reinforcers. Self-administered rewards and intrinsic reinforcement are equally important applications. That individuals do arrange conditions of reinforcement for themselves is apparent in the everyday examples of the executive who promises himself a long vacation upon completion of some project, the housewife who rewards herself with a purchase of some extravagant personal item, and the dieter who consumes an occasional ice-cream sundae as a reward for "good behavior." Not only may rewards be self-administered, but they may also grow out of intense involvement with some activity. For most individuals, there are tasks with high degrees of *intrinsic reinforcement,* tasks that "turn them on." Such activities can continue to be performed with much intensity and effort over long periods of time in the absence of external reinforcement. While it is obvious that not all organizational tasks can be so designed as to facilitate and encourage intrinsic reinforcement and self-administered rewards, it is equally obvious that much more attention can be paid to the nature of organizational work so that the intrinsic reinforcements of the job can be increased. Recent efforts to increase worker motivation through the use of job enlargement are one example of the possible importance of intrinsic reinforcement in the organizational setting. Certainly, managers can be alert to the possibility of work designs and work assignments that increase the probability of intrinsic reinforcement.

Mixed reinforcement systems

As we noted above, several cultures can exist in the same organization. The existence of multiple cultures should alert the change agent to the likelihood of several socialization processes and hence of several reinforcement systems as well. Formal organizational reward structures may compete with several informal reward structures, and it is often the case that attempts to alter organizational change will fail unless the informal reward structures are recognized and coped with. Since immediate reinforcements are far more important in influencing behavior than those more distant in time and since socializing agents in close proximity to the person are more effective than those more distant, we can expect informal reward structures to have a greater effect upon the person's behavior than formal reward structures. Since the early studies of Elton Mayo on the *social norms* of work groups and how such norms, through differential rewards and punishments (rather than a formal wage incentive system), determined how much work was actually produced it has become increasingly evident that mixed reinforcement systems within the organization are crucial to effective change.

It is obvious that organization members can reinforce one another. This peer reinforcement can serve to maintain highly desirable organizational behaviors but can equally as well serve to maintain behaviors that are not only ineffective but highly dysfunctional for the organization as a whole. Attitudes of distrust, hostility, secrecy, negativity, and so forth can arise within given subcultures, be maintained by processes of peer reinforcement, and eventually culminate in open disputes between and among organizational subcultures and in severe malfunctions of the total organization. One must often intervene directly in the socialization processes of these groups if effective organizational change is to be realized.

SOCIAL MODELS
AND ORGANIZATIONAL SOCIALIZATION

Much of the learning in organizations is *vicarious*. One need not undergo reinforcement learning in order to be influenced in the context of the organization. One can observe the behaviors of others and the outcomes of their behaviors. In effect, other persons can serve as effective *social models* (Bandura and Walters, 1963). That human beings will imitate others and pattern their behaviors, beliefs, and values after them is, of course, well recognized. As we shall see in a later portion of this chapter, there are important applications of this fact to organizational change. For the moment, however, let us briefly consider the factors associated with models and socialization.

Response consequences

People do not blindly and indiscriminately imitate the behavior of others; they choose. One factor that determines whether or not behavior displayed by a model will be performed by an observer concerns the response consequences or outcomes. When a model's behavior is perceived by the observer as leading to valued outcomes, the probability of imitative behavior on the part of the observer is increased. When the model's behavior does not lead to valued outcomes, the observer is less likely to follow his example. Hence, people will tend to imitate those behaviors that they perceive as leading to reinforcements.

Reinforcement control

Models who possess control over desired reinforcements are likely to be more effective than those who do not possess such control. The situation is most effective when the model both exhibits the behaviors to be performed and can directly reinforce imitative behaviors.

Identification, status, and prestige

Various characteristics of models have been shown to influence their effectiveness. Other things being equal, persons are more likely to be influenced by models with whom they identify. To a very significant extent, the outstanding success of various self-help groups (e.g., Alcoholic's Anonymous, Synanon, weight control groups, etc.) has been built around the fact that people are more readily influenced by those with whom they identify than by those with whom they do not. Alcoholic's Anonymous uses this approach routinely to alter one of the most difficult patterns of behavior to change, compulsive drinking. It is intriguing to note that where years of professional medical, psychiatric, and psychological treatment fail, alcoholics themselves are the best change agents available. At least part of this success is surely attributable to the fact that recovered alcoholics serve as very effective social models —models with whom other alcoholics can identify and who are seen as possessing both credibility and expertise. It often seems that models who are seen as possessing prestige and status are more effective than those who are not.

Filmed models

In order for modeling to be effective, it is not necessary that observers watch real-life action. Filmed sequences of model behavior have been effective in a variety of contexts. At least part of the recent controversy over violence in television programs stems from the realistic belief among lay persons that filmed actions can importantly influence observers (and they can).

What behaviors can be learned?

Although the range of behaviors that can be learned through the use of social models has yet to be systematically explored, there is evidence that the range is wide. Attitudes and behaviors toward members of minority groups, delinquent and nondelinquent behavior, neurotic patterns of interpersonal behavior such as aggression and dependency, moral behavior, and conformity to and violation of rules have all been shown experimentally to be influenced by social models. Even internal emotional responses have been conditioned by learning procedures involving social models.

Models and organizational cultures

As with reinforcement and socialization processes within the organization, it is clear that organizational subcultures accomplish much socialization through social models, and it is likely that those models effective in the informal cultures of the organization are not necessarily those recognized and approved by the formal culture. Often, effective models in the informal culture will display behaviors that are dysfunctional for the total organizational effort. Moreover, they are likely to receive much social reinforcement for these behaviors. As we shall see, an organization interested in altering the behaviors of its *key members* should be sure of just who those *key members* are. The effective models in the subcultures of a culturally diverse organization are not necessarily those in formal organizational positions.

DIRECT INSTRUCTION
AND ORGANIZATIONAL SOCIALIZATION

Much learning of significance for organizational functioning takes place in the many face-to-face encounters that routinely occur in the everyday life of the organization. It is in such interactions that members share impressions of the organizational environment, communicate their expectations, discuss other organizational members, and, in general, tell one another "what is really going on around here." While it might appear to the casual observer that all organizational activity is task-related, the more sophisticated observer cannot miss the surprisingly large amount of their time that members of organizations spend in exchanging information about the nature of the social system in which they find themselves. In many instances, this exchange of information takes the form of direct instruction by one organizational member of another and becomes a critical ingredient of the socialization process. This process is particularly evident in the interchanges between "old" members of an organization and "newcomers." "Old" members are seen by "newcomers" as highly credible and trustworthy observers and subsequent attitudes, expectations, and beliefs are often importantly influenced by these early interactions.

It is often useful to think of this aspect of organizational socialization in terms of *opinion leaders* and *followers*. That is, for reasons of personal charisma, organizational position, rank, seniority, and other factors, certain individuals in the organization are able to exercise considerable influence over others. They are seen by others as valuable information sources whose opinions about the nature of organizational reality are to be trusted in most matters. Once again, however, it is important to bear in mind that opinion leaders are not necessarily those persons in authority positions in the formal organization.

ORGANIZATIONAL CULTURES, SOCIALIZATION, AND ORGANIZATIONAL CHANGE

As we have seen, then, organizations can be seen as ranging in degrees of cultural uniformity from single-cultured, highly homogeneous entities to collections of several sharply differing cultures. The patterns of values, beliefs, and behaviors which make up the cultures of the organization are maintained and transmitted to new members through the process of organizational socialization. In our discussions of reinforcement, social models, and direct instruction, we have attempted to show the ingredients of the socialization process. But why should one concern himself with such apparently theoretical matters? We will try to answer this question now that some familiarity with the concepts has been gained.

Understanding and coping
with resistance to change

In his role as change agent, the manager must understand the organization as a social system. He must know where the resistances to change are likely to occur when planned change efforts are undertaken. These resistances are, in part, predictable from knowledge of the cultural mix of the organization. Certainly, there are occasions when the dominant culture of an organization clearly indicates that a particular planned change technique is totally inappropriate and exceedingly likely to fail. For example, change techniques that involve substantial degrees of interpersonal trust and cooperation are not likely to make a difference where these values are only weakly evident. Furthermore, in the case of a multiply cultured organization, the change agent must be aware of the fact that certain change techniques that might be successful with one organizational subculture might very well fail with another.

Utilizing naturally occurring
social influence

The processes we have discussed are not alien to the organization. There is ample evidence that such things as reinforcement, imitative behavior, and direct social influence are common ingredients of any social system. The change agent should be aware of the facts of organizational socialization and, where possible, bring them into the service of *planned* organizational change. People do influence one another. They do so whether a change agent, as such, is present or not. Unfortunately, though, the social influence process in the organization frequently operates to the detriment of both the individual and the organization. This fact is often overlooked by those critics who see the use of techniques such as deliberate and planned reinforcement and social modeling as manipulative and contrary to humanistic values. Why this should be so is rather puzzling. It is clear that informal and naturally occurring socialization processes can result in demands for excessive conformity, restrictions on personal freedom, interpersonal manipulation, and the learning of patterns of behavior that are disastrous for both the individual and the organization. Simply because a process occurs in an uncontrolled and therefore "natural" way is no reason to suppose that its outcomes will be beneficial to all concerned. On the other hand, one could well imagine the *deliberate* use of socialization to reinforce attitudes of trust, cooperation, and individual creativity, and to maximize in a rational way the degree of individual freedom, job satisfaction, and social satisfaction possible in a given organization.

Identifying paradoxical social influence effects

As we have noted, the managers themselves may unwittingly maintain dysfunctional organizational behaviors and prevent functional changes through inappropriate patterns of reinforcement. Moreover, formal organizational reward structures may also prevent changes in behavior necessary for effective organizational functioning. Awareness of the powerful effects of reinforcement upon behavior is the first step in recognition of paradoxical social influence effects within the organization.

Identifying key persons in the organization

Understanding of the organization as a social system aids the change agent in identifying key persons useful in the change process. While some of these persons will clearly be those in formal management positions, one may also discover persons who do not occupy positions in the formal authority structure but who are nonetheless critical in the success of a change effort. As we have seen, influential social models and opinion leaders may exist in the informal cultures of the organization as well.

APPLICATIONS OF SOCIAL LEARNING TECHNIQUES: REINFORCEMENT

We will first consider several ways in which reinforcement theory can be applied to the problem of organizational change.

Analyzing reinforcement contingencies: formal reward structures

The alert change agent should constantly monitor the organization's system of reinforcements, both formal and informal. The formal reward structure should be carefully examined and in analyzing it attention should be paid to such questions as the following:

1) Is the reward structure of the organization consistent with the overall goals of the organization? Does the formal reward structure encourage such patterns of behavior that the only ways rewards can be obtained are through behaviors that are actually dysfunctional for the larger organization?

2) Does the formal reward structure require individuals to de-emphasize certain organizational goals in favor of others?

3) Does the formal reward structure set up a situation in which destructive competitiveness both between individuals and between organizational subunits becomes a necessary condition for reward? Competitive incentive programs, in particular, must be carefully scrutinized to ensure that individual and departmental rivalries do not culminate in mutually destructive behavior.

4) Does the formal reward structure ensure that organizational changes cannot be brought about? How can the formal reward structure be altered to facilitate desired changes in behavior?

5) Is the scheduling of formal rewards optimal? Can organizational changes be brought about through lengthening or shortening the interval between reward administrations?

6) To what extent can the formal reward structure be diversified to capitalize on the individual differences in preferences for reinforcers? Other than varying the nature of reinforcers, can the formal reward structure be tailored to meet individual differences in preference for scheduling? Can some individuals or departments be paid more frequently than others? Can desired changes in organizational behavior be produced by fitting formal reward systems to individual differences?

Analyzing reinforcement contingencies: informal reward structure

The alert change agent will also analyze the informal reward structure. Data for such analyses can be generated in several ways, but perhaps the most useful is that of controlled observation of samples of behavior. Trained observers, either organizational members or outside consultants, can gather data on the nature, frequency, and occasions of rewards in the informal social system. Such observations can also yield information on those persons in the informal system who are effective reinforcing agents as well as influential social models. Once again, the change agent should address himself to certain questions:

1) Are the patterns of reinforcement in the informal cultures of the organization consistent with the goals of the formal organization?

2) Who are the influential agents in the informal structure who have control over reinforcements?

3) What are the effective reinforcers in the informal structure—recognition, status, work materials, space, privacy?

4) Does the informal reward structure encourage interpersonal and interdepartmental rivalries and dysfunctional relationships?

5) Does the informal reward structure mitigate against successful outcomes of change programs currently under way or planned?

Training effective reinforcing agents

In our interactions with others, we may often reinforce patterns of dependency, duplicity, and even hostility without realizing that we are doing so. We must not disregard this very critical aspect of interpersonal influence as trivial, even though the importance of such dysfunctional patterns of reinforcing behavior is often minimized. Managers, supervisors, and other key persons in the organization can be trained to become careful observers of their own behavior and that of others.

Such training should be directed toward producing persons who are very much aware of the behaviors they are reinforcing and of the reinforcing aspects of their own behavior. The training need not be complicated and lengthy. Since it is simple to grasp the concept of unwitting and unintended reinforcement in the abstract, but often very difficult for a person to see these *in his actual behavior,* perhaps the most effective way to conduct it is through the analysis of filmed sequences of interaction involving the persons being trained. When successful, this training can be valuable for several reasons:

1) It may produce changes in the organization by removing dysfunctional reinforcing behavior on the part of key people.

2) It may provide the necessary pool of trained people to initiate change programs based upon reinforcement theory.

3) Persons thus trained can be used to support and maintain changes in behavior brought about by other methods.

Clarifying and enriching the reinforcement environment

The central task of the change agent who chooses to adopt reinforcement techniques is that of *redesigning the reinforcement environment* of the organization. The assumption is made that if the reinforcement environment of the organization can be clarified, enriched, and brought into congruence with the goals and objectives of the organization, desirable changes in organizational behavior are likely to follow. As we have seen, the reinforcement structure of both the formal and the informal organizations must be analyzed and effective reinforcing agents must be trained. Such analysis and training is necessary if an appropriate reinforcement environment is to be accomplished.

In attempting to redesign the reinforcement environment of an organization, the change agent should ask himself the following questions:

Are reinforcement contingencies clear and unambiguous? • That is, are organizational members, both the dispensers and recipients of reinforcements, clear as to what behaviors lead to what outcomes? In many cases, the relationships between specific behaviors and possible outcomes are left vague and unspecified. Organizational members simply do not know what aspects of their behavior may be reliably expected to be reinforced. Moreover, it is often the case that reinforcing agents behave very inconsistently, sometimes rewarding a given behavior and on other occasions failing to reward or even punishing. Such ambiguity and uncertainty should be removed so that organizational members may come to hold clear expectations as to what specific behaviors are likely to lead to given specific outcomes. From this perspective, one can see that applications of reinforcement theory to the organization, rather than being a manipulative procedure, can actually be the means through which organizational members gain a measure of control over their environments. When the outcomes for given behaviors are clear and unequivocal, the person is operating in a *known* environment, one which he can control, if he wishes, by choosing to perform behaviors that will produce desired outcomes.

Are reinforcing events sufficiently varied? • Bearing in mind the facts of individual differences in preferences for reinforcers, the change agent must ensure that the reinforcement environment of the organization includes reinforcers of many different kinds. Rest periods, vacation time, social recognition, increased pay, increased space, increased privacy, increased opportunity for affiliating with other workers, fringe benefits, and special materials associated with given tasks are but a few of the many different kinds of reinforcers available within the organizational context. Organizations can and do vary considerably in the relative richness of the mix of reinforcements routinely employed. In an organization in which the range of reinforcers is narrow, an alert change agent can link desired changes in behavior to a progressively widening pool of valued outcomes.

Are reinforcers present in sufficient numbers? • Studies by one of the authors (Wallace, unpublished) of the elementary school as a social organization revealed the interesting fact that classrooms varied widely in the sheer number of reinforcements available. Some classroom teachers were *low rate* reinforcing agents, dispensing very few reinforcers over the course of a day of interaction in the classroom. Other teachers were *high rate* reinforcing agents in that they reinforced students almost constantly throughout the school day. The results suggested that, in considering the question of frequency of reinforcement, one must take care to ensure that reinforcements are not so scarce as to convince members that their attainment is exceedingly improbable. On the other hand, when reinforcers are easy to obtain, their reinforcing value is likely to decrease. That is, the relationship between the value of an outcome and its probability of occurrence is not a simple, straightforward linear relationship.

Is appropriate behavior being reinforced? • This is perhaps the most critical question of all from the perspective of reinforcement theory. In designing the reinforcement environment of the organization, the change agent must take care to ensure that organizationally desired, rather than dysfunctional, behaviors are being reinforced.

Are the scheduling and timing of reinforcements optimal? •

Finally, the change agent should consider the questions involving scheduling and timing of reinforcements. As a general rule, immediate reinforcements are far more effective than delayed ones. There are, however, individual differences. A change agent should experiment with a variety of reinforcement schedules in the context of a particular organization and observe the outcomes. The best approach to follow is probably that of frequent and consistent reinforcements in the early phases of learning new patterns of behavior, gradually shifting to a pattern of intermittent reinforcement on some fixed or variable basis.

Maximizing intrinsic reinforcement

In some cases, successful changes can be brought about through the analysis and redesign of work. When such changes can increase the intrinsic reinforcement of the work itself, the situation is ideal. In his role as change agent, the manager should be ever cognizant of the possibility that changes in the nature of the tasks that organizational members perform can be an effective vehicle for other changes as well. Aside from directly altering tasks, the manager may take advantage of the possible increases in intrinsic reinforcement through assignment and reassignment. In some instances, it may prove feasible for workers to participate in the actual design of work. When workers are given the opportunity to exercise some control over the characteristics of their jobs, greater commitment, involvement, and intrinsic satisfactions may be among the outcomes. Recent experience with job enlargement (widening the nature of the job and extending worker responsibility accordingly) seems, under certain conditions, to be accompanied by changes in job satisfaction and motivation. Of course, it is not always possible to alter job characteristics or to involve everyone in the design of work, but change agents should be on the lookout for situations amenable to such interventions.

APPLICATIONS OF SOCIAL LEARNING TECHNIQUES: THE USE OF MODELS

Social models, as we have seen, can strikingly affect the behavior of observers. There is no reason that this fact should be ignored in seeking ways to produce changes in the organizational context. In this section, we will briefly consider some deliberate and planned uses of social models in facilitating change.

Selecting models

Influential persons from both the formal and informal cultures are prime candidates for selection. The identification of potential models can be accomplished through the use of various *reputation measures,* questionnaires that ask organizational members to pinpoint the "influential persons" in their work environments. Measures that clearly get at *identification* of one person with another could also be used. Observations in actual working situations are still another way in which persons with modeling potential can be identified.

Reinforcing models for appropriate behaviors

In some instances, it is possible to reinforce directly those persons who consistently display organizationally desirable attributes. In the case of *key* people who frequently display organizationally dysfunctional behaviors, it may prove possible to alter their behavior by selectively reinforcing functional behaviors while ignoring other behaviors. In general, however, the purpose of reinforcing the model is to display clearly to observers the relationship between specific behaviors and valued outcomes.

Training models in appropriate behaviors

Wherever possible, deliberate training programs should be undertaken. In the case of management training, the modeling aspects of behavior should be routinely stressed. Obviously, one of the functions of the manager as a change agent is to display consistently and clearly— to set an example of—the attributes and characteristics he would like to see come about in the organization. Once again, it is important to point out that such training need not produce dull, gray, conforming, "organization men." An effective social model in a creative and dynamic organization could very well be counted upon to display such things as effective problem-solving strategies, forceful decision-making behaviors, respect for individuals, tolerance for other ways to approach a task, flexibility, trust, cooperation, and empathy.

The training of effective models, however, should not stop with key people from management but should be conducted at all levels of the organization. An interesting but rarely attempted strategy for organizational change would be to train models from all levels of the organization in a careful and deliberate manner, thereby "seeding" the organization with visible, effective, dynamic persons who do not simply talk about how the organization should be and how it should be changed but who actually *enact* these visions for all to see in the day-to-day functioning of the organization.

Filmed models

The use of carefully planned and constructed filmed presentations of modeled behavior can prove valuable in both management and worker training programs. Not only have they been shown to serve as effective examples, but they can easily be employed routinely as a part of specific organizational change programs. An interesting possibility would be for organizations to take on the responsibility of producing their own films in which problems specific to the organization are depicted, solutions are presented, and actual managers and workers are used as the actors. While at first blush this might appear terribly extravagant, a well designed "home" film series might well yield benefits far in excess of the costs.

OFFSETTING THE EFFECTS
OF DYSFUNCTIONAL PEER
SOCIALIZATION

In dealing with the direct instruction of organizational members by one another, the change agent should take advantage of the effects of peer socialization processes. Much of the "scuttlebutt" in organizations arises precisely because communications are inadequate, people feel left out of things generally, and the far-reaching effects of the informal socialization process are unrecognized. Gossip, rumor, distorted perceptions, and even organizational "paranoia" are the natural outcomes of an organizational communications system characterized by much upper-level secrecy and generally limited participation. The uncertainty and anxiety generated by such systems make it inevitable that people will turn to other people at their level of the organization for information about the organizational environment, confirmation of their beliefs and suspicions, and so forth. Of course, there is nothing inherently wrong in such sharing of beliefs and opinions among peers. It is a natural characteristic, to some extent, of all organizations. However, when the informal socialization process produces and maintains distorted perceptions of the organization and highly dysfunctional behaviors as well it obviously must be changed. In general, the unwanted effects of dysfunctional peer socialization can be offset by techniques that involve opening up communications across all levels of the organization. "New member" orientation programs that "really tell it like it is" can prove invaluable for eliminating the necessity for new members to rely exclusively on the perceptions of a few influential older members for information as to the nature of organizational realities. Management can at least make certain that "opinion leaders" in the organization are in possession of accurate information. But, in the final analysis, appropriate patterns of peer socialization are characteristic of organizations with high degrees of interpersonal trust, open communications, collaborative interaction, cooperation, and generally supportive interaction. In subsequent pages, we will discuss techniques for producing changes in these desirable directions.

SUMMARY

In this chapter, we have discussed the important ideas and applications derived from social learning theory. Although many of the ideas may seem quite obvious and perhaps even trivial, the change agent should not take them lightly. There is ample evidence for one to believe that social learning factors are critical in the functioning of any organization. They are certainly too potent to be ignored.

REFERENCES

Bandura, A., and R. H. Walters. *Social Learning and Personality Development.* Holt, Rinehart & Winston, 1963.
Lawrence, P. R., and J. W. Lorsch. *Organization and Environment:*

Managing Differentiation and Integration. Harvard Business
   School, 1967.
Schmidt, W. H. *Organizational Frontiers and Human Values.* Wads-
   worth, 1970.
Ullmann, L. P. *Institution and Outcome.* Pergamon, 1967.

The Laboratory Approach to Change

5

Laboratory method, or laboratory training, as it is sometimes called, grew out of several major concerns of social scientists.[1] These concerns centered about the nature of education for effective social relationships and about the development of an *applied* behavioral science which would utilize scientific data for the attainment of socially desirable and significant goals. The rapid development of the laboratory approach is attributable to the feelings of urgency among social scientists and practicing managers for the cultivation of new and improved methods for facilitating planned organizational change.

The origins of laboratory training can be traced to the work of Kurt Lewin and others who were interested in experimental approaches to the study of group function. During a program for teaching individual and group skills to enhance productivity, his staff inadvertently discovered that the small group was potentially a potent learning device. By allowing unstructured groups to develop and by using the group as a subject for analysis, they found that individuals learned much about their own behavior, the behavior of others, and group behavior as well. Thus the T-group (T for training), destined to grow to some stature as a vehicle for planned change, was born. Laboratory method is rightly associated with the National Training Laboratories which held their first laboratory training session in Bethel, Maine, in 1947.

1. *The material in this chapter draws heavily from Bradford et al., 1964; Marrow, 1964; and Schein and Bennis, 1965.*

The approach is relatively new, still growing and changing. Many issues and debates over its use and usefulness have been generated, and most of these are still unresolved (Odiorne, 1963; Campbell and Dunnette, 1968).

In this chapter the concept of laboratory method is discussed. Some variations in laboratory training are described and some aspects of laboratory training which need to be considered by the practicing manager are outlined.

WHAT IS LABORATORY TRAINING?

To understand laboratory training one must first understand the underlying framework within which the training takes place. Although there are variations in the content, the design, the time period in which the training can take place, and the specific objectives that the training can focus on, there is nevertheless an underpinning of characteristics which all laboratory training programs have in common.

Laboratory learning

The laboratory learning model deviates from the more traditional teacher-student approach which focuses primarily on intellectual learning. Laboratory training attempts to integrate traditional educational elements such as lectures, theory building, and analysis with an experiential or affective component. Traditional learning models have assumed that increased knowledge would inevitably result in behavior change. Laboratory method questions this assumption and provides an experiential component aimed at helping the learner translate his knowledge into appropriate and effective action. The ability of the individual to apply what he knows in situations of ambiguity, stress, and tension requires an approach to learning which includes more activities than the traditional classroom situation. Hence, laboratory education is both intellectual and experiential.

The action research model

Laboratory training is change oriented. The approach is aimed at helping participants become more aware of their own perceptions and attitudes, and to understand how these things influence their behavior. The opportunity to act, evaluate those actions, and take new action is provided in the laboratory setting. The experience provides the individual with the basis for developing hypotheses about individual behavior, interpersonal behavior, and group phenomena. And most importantly, he can test these hypotheses through action in the group, modifying them or even devising new ones for test in further action.

The group as subject and resource

The process of laboratory education involves the utilization of the training group as a self-analytic body. Group members use the group as the subject matter of discussions involving talk about themselves, about their behavior in relation to others, or about reactions to group processes and procedures. To facilitate this process emphasis is placed on the "here and now" approach. The focus for material to be explored comes from the *experience* of the participants. This emphasis provides a common arena in which the material that is diagnosed and discussed is generated by individuals in the training setting. The advantages of focusing upon present experience are that it permits participants to use real and commonly experienced events as data, it provides a basis for generating theory and concepts that can be directly linked to experience, and it helps to create a supportive group climate which in turn increases the person's willingness to examine his own behavior and risk experimenting with change.

Unstructured setting

The laboratory training setting is conducive to learning new patterns of behavior. When the familiar structures and mechanisms of everyday life are suspended as they are in the training group, there is a necessity for individuals to search for and create their own structures. Making sense out of the ambiguity of the situation provides an opportunity for participants to test out and examine their personal styles and behaviors. Critical analysis of usual patterns of behavior and the search for new patterns are more likely in the training situation than in the real-life setting where people are apt to employ unthinkingly those patterns of behavior they have learned and internalized in the past.

The learner as a determinant
of the learning

The laboratory method is essentially a matter of "learning how to learn." It involves the ability of each learner to analyze his own processes of learning continuously. In addition he develops his own personal resources to use his environment, including other people, to learn about the ways in which he might behave more effectively in particular situations. In this way laboratory training is indeed a process of reeducation. The learner is apt to find himself in situations in which he has to give up many values, attitudes, and sets of behaviors that he has learned in the past but which are no longer functional.

Laboratory training stresses the notion that each participant is the best judge both of what interests him most and of the way in which he most effectively learns. The laboratory method permits variations in the way in which individuals learn and the array of things that are possible for individuals to learn. The participant guides and directs his own learning process with help and support from others.

In essence then, laboratory education tries to integrate the intellectual and affective components in learning. Its aim is to create an attitude toward learning which encourages individuals and organizations to assess their behavior continually and to explore alternative actions when necessary. The basic group technique has the underlying values of scientific inquiry, expanded individual choice, collaboration, and constructive conflict resolution. These values guide the design of laboratory experiences and provide a framework for the utilization of the technology of laboratory training.

VARIETY OF LABORATORY
TRAINING EMPHASES

The best way of describing the variety of learning possibilities via the laboratory method is to do so in terms of the major goals toward which laboratory experiences are directed. The content focus of the laboratory can be organized to emphasize learning about the self, the self in relation to others, group and intergroup phenomena, and the larger dimensions of organizations and communities. In any given laboratory, any one of these may be the central focus for learning.

Personal development laboratories

In this instance the content of learning is aimed largely at providing individuals with an opportunity to become more aware of their own behavior. The focus is primarily personal with the *self* being the focus of attention. The laboratory design permits an exploration and diagnosis of behavior via feedback from others. The purpose is for each individual to understand more fully what he is doing, how he is doing it, and to encourage the development of options for behavior change. Exercises which the individual can engage in, either alone or with others, are often used to facilitate the learning. Training experiences of this kind are usually designed for "strangers"—people who do not normally have relationships with each other outside of the laboratory setting.

Human relations laboratory

Laboratories of this type (the T-group and the encounter group) focus on exploring and understanding the nature of interpersonal relations. Participants are given opportunities for the generation of interpersonal data, diagnosis of the interpersonal situation, and for the development of skills for enhancing communication, creating interpersonal rapport, providing help in interpersonal problem-solving, and resolving interpersonal conflict.

Participants in these laboratories can be from "stranger" populations or they can be people from the same organization. More and more training of this sort has been initiated in organizations, not only as a way of developing increased interpersonal competence, but as a vehicle for building interpersonal ties among people who have some working relationship. Such designs can involve a diagonal slice of the organization or a horizontal slice. In either case the training does not include participants who are in a direct superior-subordinate relationship. These designs are most useful when the major laboratory goal is personal and interpersonal learning in general, rather than organizationally oriented learning.

Group dynamics laboratory

In this instance the focus is on group phenomena and the participant learns to diagnose and intervene in group processes. Exercises can be utilized to explore group decision-making, group problem-solving, the ways in which group structures and cultures develop, techniques for changing group norms, and how groups might organize to accomplish specific tasks. The focus is the study of the developing character of the group and ways in which that character can be analyzed ("process analysis") and changed through the actions of the group members.

Organizational laboratories

Organizational laboratories are designed to deal with larger organizational systems. The content for laboratories of this type might focus on the relationships between groups, the causes and resolution of organizational conflict, or the process of goal formation. Organizational laboratories, which could involve up to 100 people, can simulate a variety of organizational configurations and analyze the consequences of each design.

As is common with laboratory education in general, time can be spent both in theory building to help understand the emerging phenomena, and on individual and group skill development in coping with the problems of the simulated organization. Laboratories of this kind have been used successfully in organization settings, for example, as a learning device to prepare members for an organizational merger.

The instrumented laboratory

The instrumented laboratory derives its name from the extensive use of "instruments" such as questionnaires, tapes, and video recordings to generate data and facilitate the learning process. Instrumented laboratories can be conducted with or without a trainer. The emphasis is very much on experimentation and on the "quantitative" representation of the group processes. Participants are encouraged to play the roles of subjects, observers, analysts, interpreters, and consultants. The trainer may play a role in providing instruction in methods of dealing with the data, techniques of analysis, and theory in interpretation.

The use of instruments provides a basis for analyzing the progress of the group. Quantitative data from such instruments may be useful in detecting those more subtle aspects of group behavior which may go unrecognized in unstructured groups. Organizations may benefit from the instrumented approach since there are certain economies associated with the method—fewer trainers are required, the organization's own people can be trained in using the instrument, and fewer training sessions may be required. Instrumented laboratories are often less anxiety producing in format. Moreover, the data gathered and analyzed can have multiple organizational uses, such as for the design of management training sessions.

Teams and team laboratories

Organizational teams often find it useful to use laboratories to focus on the individual learning that appears in the context of working directly on real organizational problems. Laboratory learning can have direct impact on the operations of the team involved. The subject matter for the team's discussion would be the "real life" issues, problems, and dilemmas the team is experiencing. The learning inputs and laboratory design would be aimed at helping the group identify the issues more clearly as well as to generate solutions. The outcomes of such laboratories are twofold: one, there is immediate payoff by sharpening the present operating procedures of the team; and two, skills for dealing with such problems in the future are likely to be developed.

ROLE OF THE LABORATORY TRAINER

Although it is difficult to assess the nature of the impact of the laboratory trainer on the learning outcomes, his behavior is indeed an important factor (Tannenbaum, et al., 1961). The specific ways in which he can influence the learning process are by:

Modeling behavior

The trainer can influence the development of appropriate learning norms by personal example. Although each trainer has a unique style and approach, each nevertheless tries to demonstrate the ways in which openness and authenticity can be useful dimensions for personal learning. In some instances the trainer may help establish this norm by being open and expressive himself—by sharing his feelings or by interjecting observations about group processes. The trainer's particular stance is a product of his own theory of laboratory learning and of his own personal characteristics. The goal, however, remains the same: to encourage by demonstration the development of group norms that bear directly on the climate for learning.

Providing inputs of concepts and theory

The trainer can provide the appropriate intellectual base to help participants understand and diagnose the interpersonal and group phenomena that emerge in the laboratory setting.

Pushing the boundaries

Another kind of behavior that the trainer may exhibit involves the removal of the traditional social amenities and structures with which participants are familiar. In so doing, he creates situations which, by the novelty and ambiguity of their stimulation, force the participant to act. In this way new situations can be confronted, reactions analyzed, and alternative approaches experimented with.

Providing support in facilitating change

The trainer can provide support as individuals discover new behavior and attitudes to integrate into their personal styles. Although all participants can potentially play a supportive role, the trainer's special expertise and experience is vital in making the group aware of the difference between support and *protection*. Although we may think we are giving support to other persons, we may, in reality, be protecting them from fully experiencing the necessary stress and discomfort that often accompany significant learning about the self.

Stimulating confrontation

The potential for growth and learning is probably best realized through a process of self-confrontation. The confrontative aspect of the trainer's role deserves special attention. The laboratory approach tends to focus on the development of a supportive-trusting climate as a necessary condition for learning. Some important learning, however, may take place under seemingly quite opposite conditions. Anxiety, stress, and tension may produce as much significant learning as does the support-trust model. Learning to cope with frustration, aggression, and the like can be important in the present turmoil of our society. The trainer must be able to assess which situation, support-trust or anxiety-tension, is likely to produce significant learning for the group and for each individual. Although the trainer is not interested in master-minding the participant's education, he can rarely, if ever, assume a completely passive role. One of his functions is to create opportunities for learning in a variety of ways appropriate to the situation. The ability to provide opportunities for self-confrontation is an important dimension of the trainer's role.

LABORATORY LEARNING
APPLIED TO ORGANIZATIONAL LIFE

The training laboratory, especially the T-group or encounter group, has created a good deal of controversy. Its critics argue that T-groups have not produced any observable lasting change in attitudes or behavior. Some even contend that T-groups, especially those used in organizations, can create undesirable and damaging effects for the organization (House, 1969), but despite inconclusive research data, the laboratory method is gaining the support of more and more people in all types of organizations. The promise of this method as a potential vehicle for introducing and implementing change is stimulating more and more experimentation and study.

Initially, it may appear that laboratory training is an intense personal experience, but an experience separate from the demands of day-to-day living, and especially those of organizational life. Yet submerged in what appears to be a deluge of personal experiences, events, reactions, and feelings are some important things that have direct relevance to the organizational roles of managers. We will consider these organizationally relevant matters here.

Understanding and skill in group development

In most organizations the development of effective work groups and managerial teams is becoming more and more a necessity. The newly formed work group or team is confronted early with the problems of group building. Dealing with the differential requirements of members, as well as with the group goals, even implicit goals, is a situation which faces each laboratory participant and each manager. A specific and frequent training session problem, illustrative of this point, is the issue of participation. In organizational terms it is analogous to the problem of contribution. How does a manager motivate each team member to maximum contribution? How does the manager cope with the issues of responsibility and individual accountability? The discomfort of team members during discussions of accountability is reminiscent of discussions of participation in training sessions. Effective teams must deal with the issues of groupness *versus* individuality and autonomy *versus* interdependence. The unique integration of group demands and individual needs is characteristic of successful managerial teams as well as effective laboratory training sessions. The training situation provides a rich opportunity to confront and cope with a common organizational issue.

Understanding and dealing with authority

One kind of possible learning opportunity in the training situation stems from the trainer's refusal to accept and act in a traditional authority role. The result is an "authority vacuum." Efforts by factions of the group to impose an authority system are met with resistance and these attempts seem to fall by the wayside rather quickly. The sudden awareness by the group of the dimensionality of the authority problem and its relation to individual prerogatives can produce profound learning about some troublesome organizational problems. To what extent does authority impose restriction on individual freedom? How do perceived threats to freedom affect individual behavior? Can individuals find a way to "do their own thing" in the context of organizational life? What alternatives are there when those organization demands which restrict individual freedom also constrain individual contribution?

Understanding and dealing with ambiguity and uncertainty

Modern-day organizations are faced with such a dynamic and rapidly changing environment that there is a great demand on the manager to cope with ambiguities and uncertainties. Managerial effectiveness in the future depends largely on the manager's personal sense of confidence and trust in himself. Practice in coping with unstructured and undefined situations may develop in the manager a capacity to generate his own information and to make creative sense out of a vague and nebulous situation.

Understanding personal revitalization

Among others, two of the goals of laboratory training are to provide each individual with insights into his own personal learning profile—the way in which he learns best—and to create positive attitudes toward continual learning and development.

The current attention to the processes and methods of organizational change must be matched with equal attention to the processes of individual manager development. The traditional approaches to management training are incomplete attempts to develop managers who are capable of coping with the complex demands of contemporary organizations, but recent contention has it that individual manager training does little to facilitate organizational change. The trend has been to conceptualize training in terms of the "system." The evidence to support "organizational or system training," as an avenue toward organizational change, is equally as sparse. From our perspective, both appear to be necessary. Regardless of the advances that may occur in a system approach, there is clearly a pressing need for a technology that provides real and meaningful opportunities for *individual managers* to *change*. No real organizational change can occur without personal change on the part of key administrators. Laboratory training is a step in this direction.

MANAGEMENT DECISIONS IN THE USE OF LABORATORY TRAINING

Laboratory training can be an extremely potent vehicle for change. There are, however, a number of decision areas the manager must concern himself with when considering the use of laboratory training in his organization.

Choosing appropriate content

It is important that the objectives, content, and design of the particular laboratory session be appropriate to the situation. The manager should consider both the nature of the changes he wishes to see occur in his organization and specific ways in which these can be accomplished through the laboratory approach. Diagnosis of his organization's needs and the relationship of those needs to the potential outcomes of laboratory training is an important area of concern. Laboratory training takes time, money, and other resources; the usual format is an intense experience in which members of the organization may be away from their jobs for an extended period of time. The manager must seriously question whether there may not be other more appropriate ways of introducing and bringing about change.

Choice of staff

The manager must consider the choice of staff as an important ingredient in the success of the program. The laboratory staff should be selected on the basis of their expertise and experience in the particular areas which are the focus of the laboratory training session. It can be advantageous if the laboratory staff have at least a cursory understanding of the organization, its tasks and outputs, and the environment in which it functions. It is obvious that such information can facilitate the design of the laboratory training and can significantly influence the content.

Readiness of the organization

Laboratory training is based on a set of values which emphasize openness, collaboration, and the expression of feelings. It may be that the organizational culture is so at odds with the values of the training laboratory that the method is simply not feasible. The collaborative aspects and personal nature of laboratory training imply that interpersonal phenomena are both necessary and appropriate as subjects for discussion, particularly when they are essential or germane to the task. In instances where the organization has strong norms against the discussion of the interpersonal dimensions, and where interpersonal expression is dealt with in punitive ways, the appropriateness of organizationally oriented laboratory training would be in question.

Interdependence of organizational segments

The manager must give careful thought to the impact of laboratory training on other groups with which his own unit may have important relationships. Conscientious planning must be done to ensure that the outcomes of laboratory training are communicated to other relevant groups and are used to change relationships in useful and worthwhile ways. Conflicts, differences, and problems can be anticipated and overcome when they are carefully thought out and dealt with openly.

Involvement of key people

People who are to be participants in laboratory training should be informed as fully as possible about the nature of the program, what is expected of them, and what kinds of outcomes are likely to occur. To be successful the laboratory training program should be supported by key people in the organization and those people should hold, in general, the attitudes and values which are compatible with the laboratory training approach. It may be necessary for the manager considering the use of laboratory training to provide some education about what the laboratory method, in its format and process, is.

An orientation prior to a laboratory program is aimed at reducing the level of anxiety and resistance toward laboratory training and its learning process. Too often attitudes about laboratory training are based on little or no information and tend to be distortions of the "real thing." The degree to which these distortions can be corrected will directly affect the nature of the laboratory training experience, its learning outcomes, and its impact on the organization.

Question of voluntarism

The optimum utilization of laboratories occurs when participants can attend on a voluntary basis. Most of the benefits from laboratory training occur when participants feel they are not being coerced, pushed, or manipulated into the experience. Although involuntary attendance is particularly hard to avoid in cases where laboratory programs are a key vehicle for change in the organization, it is nevertheless important that the organization allow as much choice as possible. This can be partially accomplished by providing individuals with an adequate orientation to laboratory process and an accurate representation of the process. The rest depends on the amount of trust and confidence people have in the proponents of the program.

Future planning

As stated previously, the success of laboratory method as a vehicle for initiating or implementing changes in an organization requires the participation of key managerial personnel. The greater the participation the more changes in attitudes and behavior can be induced at many levels in the organization, and the more the conflicts and resistance to change can be minimized. The manager thinking about using the laboratory method approach should also carefully consider ways in which people from other segments of the organization, particularly the levels above and below him, may be involved in the learning process. Laboratory training is but one element (though a significant one) in an organizational change effort. Other programs and activities need to be coordinated and integrated into an overall plan for change.

Transfer of laboratory learning

A major concern for the manager must be the problem of transfer of laboratory learning to the organizational setting. So far, several approaches have been developed to ensure that connections between laboratory learning and the organizational environment can be made by the participants. One approach is to design into the laboratory experience a significant portion of time (maybe a third of the total time) to be spent on concrete back-home problems, to let theory and experience from the T-group be used to help participants deal with real problems in a creative manner. Another approach, used when participants are from the same organization, is to conduct follow-up training sessions. These sessions, of only a few hours' duration, focus on the application of laboratory training to commonly experienced organizational problems (e.g., employee counseling). The number of sessions is not fixed and depends on the content and design of the meetings. Follow-up sessions must be planned, however, and are not for the sole purpose of renewing acquaintances. The best orientation for these sessions, vis-à-vis organizational change, is that they be problem-oriented sessions and deal specifically with the application of the laboratory experience to "real" work-related problems.

SUMMARY AND EXAMPLES

The laboratory approach is epitomized by the action-research model of action, feedback, evaluation, and action. There are a variety of laboratory experiences designed to integrate the intellectual and affective components of the learning process. Although the content may be different, the aim is the same: to increase the probability of behavioral and attitudinal change of the participants. Laboratory training can be used as a significant component in an organizational change program provided the T-group learning is transferred to the work situation. Clearly, laboratory training alone does not ensure organizational change. The question to be addressed is not "Is laboratory training good or bad?" but "How can laboratory training be managed and conducted such that organizations can benefit fully from a technology that clearly shows much promise for producing the necessary changes in individual behavior that must accompany organizational change?"

Case A

An elementary-school district decided to change both the "traditional orientation" to the task of teaching and its organizational structure. The change involved the formation of teaching teams, the establishment of resource centers within each school, and modular curriculum scheduling. During the initial stages of the change in the *technical system* of this organization, difficulties arose because of the inability of teachers and administrators to deal constructively with interpersonal difficulties. As a result, the productive collaboration so necessary in the new system was at a minimum. Primarily, the behavior of people was still geared to the old technical system. When the new system was put into effect the initial planning for change did not take into account the ability of people to function in the new technical arrangement.

A district program director initiated several laboratory training programs in which the participants were both administrators and teachers. The participants in these groups were basically "strangers," that is, from different schools. In the initial phase of the laboratory program care was taken to select people who did not work directly with one another. The thrust of the training was toward the development of interpersonal skills and the use of methods and techniques for the resolution of conflict.

In the second phase of the training program, a team building approach was used in which teacher teams, along with the appropriate administrators, met in team development sessions to focus on their own processes.

These sessions were not conducted until at least half of the team had participated in the phase one skill development program. The laboratory experience was clearly useful and contributed to the productivity of the team development sessions.

Case B

A large organization which had been using laboratory training on a wide scale became suddenly aware of the difficulties in the application of laboratory training to on-the-job situations. Participants reported that the laboratory training was a new and different kind of learning, but that its usefulness in their jobs was vague and ill defined. In an attempt to deal creatively with this issue the organization experimented with the formation of organizational clusters of participants in laboratory training programs. The clusters were made up of people who did not work directly with one another, but who *did* have potential interfaces in the pursuance of their organizational tasks. People who wished to take part in a laboratory training session were asked to recruit from three to five other persons to make a cluster. For example, one such group was made up of a representative from each of the departments of the Management Systems Division. The departments normally pursued their own special area of interest and rarely collaborated, even when issues cut across all departments.

During the laboratory training sessions time was allotted so that these organizational clusters could meet. Their task was specifically to think through and plan how the application of laboratory learning could be used to enhance their organization's effectiveness. Related clusters also met to provide additional ideas and insights for each other.

In phase two of this program, the organizational clusters continued to meet after the laboratory training program was completed. Meetings were held back in the organization to continue planning for the application of what they had learned. Most clusters identified at least one problem area to work on and actually designed and implemented a change intervention for their organization. The cluster turned out to be a useful device for helping organizations transfer laboratory learning to back-home situations. It also emphasized that laboratory training must be followed by other organizational interventions if change is to occur.

Case C

An agency of the federal government was experiencing difficulties in its operation—low morale and a backlog of orders were two of the more pressing problems. The top management of the organization decided that the problems had become so critical that diagnosis and analysis of the situation were required, along with some significant changes in the way the agency went about its business.

The initial assessment of management and their organizational consultants was that the involvement of organizational members in the change effort would be most difficult. For the most part, people were highly resistant to change, primarily because they were uncertain about its implications for themselves, and secondarily because these implications could not be discussed openly in the climate of suspicion, distrust, and destructive competitiveness that then prevailed.

As a way of approaching the problem, a management-consultant team identified those organizational members that would be most receptive to change and could potentially develop skills in facilitating the diagnostic and change process. These members were asked, on a voluntary basis, to participate in "stranger" type laboratory experiences as a way of helping them develop the necessary interpersonal and collaborative skills. About 20 percent of the organization was included in this group—about 40 of the 200 men in the organization. People were selected so that all levels of the organization were represented.

This first phase was primarily concerned with providing people in the organization with the skills necessary to cope with the problems of introducing change into the organization. At the conclusion of this phase, a team development laboratory was conducted for all management personnel. The laboratory design included different team configurations so that each manager, who was in fact a member of a number of different managerial teams (as a superior and as a subordinate), could participate in each of the groups to which he belonged. The management teams began a process of identifying the critical issues related to the total overall performance of the organization, as well as the difficulties in the operation of their own team. Initial plans were developed to implement changes in troublesome areas. Each manager also prepared to involve his subordinates, people at the working level, in diagnostic and planning activities.

As a result of the team development activity, several task groups were established to evolve new procedures and methods of operation. From these early team development sessions and the work of the initial task forces, new task forces emerged to deal with such things as reorganization of the agency, a new format for the work flow, and a reevaluation of the mission and goals of the organization. The task force format is one this organization has learned to use effectively in ongoing diagnostic and change activities.

REFERENCES

Bradford, L. P., J. R. Gibb, and K. D. Benne, eds. *T-Group Theory and Laboratory Method: Innovation in Education.* Wiley, 1964.

Campbell, J. P., and M. D. Dunnette. "Effectiveness of T-group experiences in managerial training and development." *Psychological Bulletin* 70 (August 1968): 73–104.

House, R. J. "T-group training: good or bad?" *Business Horizons* 12 (December 1969): 66–77.

Marrow, Alfred. *Behind the Executive Mask: Greater Managerial Competence Through Deeper Self-Understanding.* American Management Association, 1964.

Odiorne, G. "The trouble with sensitivity training." *Journal of American Society of Training Directors* 17 (1963): 9–20.

Schein, E. H., and W. G. Bennis. *Personal and Organizational Growth Through Group Method: The Laboratory Approach.* Wiley, 1965.

Tannenbaum, R., I. R. Weschler, and F. Massarik. *Leadership and Organization,* Chapter 9. McGraw-Hill, 1961.

Applications of
Role Theory

6

"All the world's a stage,
And all the men and women merely players;
They have their exits and entrances;
And one man in his time plays many parts . . ."

In this speech from the second act of *As You Like It*, Shakespeare anticipated much of sociological theory. That Shakespeare would stumble upon the theatrical analogy for the real-life struggles of human beings is not surprising. His own life was intensely involved with the make-believe world of actors, actresses, performances, audiences, and so forth. That he would come to see life itself as a stage with entering and exiting players is understandable. And it is equally understandable that many who have devoted their lives to the study of social behavior have come to see useful similarities between actors in the real world and those on stage. One sociologist, Erving Goffman (1959), has virtually exhausted the analogy with a detailed theory of social behavior that includes both the "onstage" and "backstage" behavior of actors, performances, costumes and props, audiences, and so on. And before Goffman, J. L. Moreno, the psychotherapist, was busily exploring the practical implications of the theatrical analogy in his *psychodrama* (Moreno, 1946), a form of psychotherapy in which persons literally act out their difficulties in company with other actors and before an audience.

83

Underlying the theatrical analogy is the concept of *role,* one which has enjoyed considerable popularity among generations of sociologists. While role concepts have been extensively utilized in sociological theory for some time, it has been only recently that widespread interest in their practical applications has appeared. In particular, it has become evident that changes in attitude and behavior can be brought about through the use of such techniques. While the reasons for such change remain a matter of debate, a wide variety of studies indicate that if a person can be induced to play a role publicly, changes in both beliefs and behavior may appear. A recent study by Mann and Janis is representative (Mann and Janis, 1968): Heavy smokers were required to play the role of cancer patients in a one-hour session in the laboratory. An experimenter acted out the role of physician. During this hour of role-playing, the heavy smokers acted out scenes in the "physician's" office in which the pain of lung cancer was focused upon, hospitalization was considered, and the certainty of early death was made evident. Changes in the numbers of cigarettes smoked over an 18-month period continued to show decreases in the role-playing group in comparison with a control group that did not have the role-playing experience.

In this chapter, we will examine the usefulness of role theory for behavior change within the context of the organization. We will first present some of the more important concepts in role theory and then examine the techniques which derive from these concepts.

CENTRAL CONCEPTS

In order to understand role theory, it is essential that we have a firm grasp on a small number of important concepts. Let us consider these briefly.

Position

The actors in a given social structure occupy highly formalized and clearly specified *positions.* In an industrial organization, for example, one may occupy the position of "middle management trainee." In other cases, positions may be a product of the informal organizational structure and a given individual may come to occupy the position of "mediator of conflicts" within a given work group. While this position is nowhere evident on the formal organizational chart, it is very real in the informal organization.

Norms

Positions carry with them expectations for the behavior of the persons who occupy them. These expectations are *norms,* prescriptions as to how the person is to behave in a given position.

Role performance

The actual behavior of the person in a given position is considered his *role performance.*

Role reciprocal

Role performance is as much a function of the persons with whom the actor interacts as of the actor himself. One cannot act in isolation from others and an adequate role performance depends, in part, upon the willingness and ability of others to assume *reciprocal roles.* It is, for example, impossible to perform adequately in the role of "supervisor" if others will not or cannot assume the reciprocal role of "supervisee." Roles and role reciprocals, then, comprise the mutual expectations and adaptations that people bring to their interactions.

Role conflict

Situations are common in which the expectations for a given position are incompatible with one another. A person is expected to do one thing while he may also be expected to do another thing that conflicts. For example, a foreman who must deal with the expectations that he get the work out and be a nice guy may find himself in a situation of role conflict. Such *role conflicts* can be the source of intense dissatisfaction and considerable tension for many persons in the organization.

Role ambiguity

When the expectations for a given position are vague and poorly formulated, a situation of *role ambiguity* exists. The actor in a given position may be uncertain of how he is to behave and others may be unsure of what their behavior should be toward him.

Role overload

It is often the case that actors may be required to perform a very complex role (one involving a large number of expectations) or perform several different roles. In either case a condition of *role overload* is said to exist. Tension and strain are characteristic problems associated with role overload and may result in poor performance.

ROLE ANALYSIS: THE PRELIMINARY STEP

The initial stages of a role theory approach to change should center upon an analysis of the constellations of role relationships that currently exist within the organization or some portion of it. This analysis may be conducted by means of the techniques for facilitating change. For example, one may learn a great deal about role relationships through role-playing simulations. Other techniques, however, may be used as well. Information generated from questionnaire studies and interviews can be used as a basis for role analysis. One can, for example, have supervisors describe their expectations for their own behavior and the behavior of those they supervise. Supervised personnel could be asked for their expectations concerning the supervisor's and their own behavior. Careful analysis of the sets of expectations revealed should show such things as conflicting and ambiguous expectations, failure of role performance, and absence of role reciprocal behavior, as well as other sources of performance difficulty.

UTILIZING THE RESULTS OF A ROLE ANALYSIS: VERBAL CLARIFICATION AND FEEDBACK

Perhaps the least complicated means for inducing change following a carefully conducted role analysis is that of verbal clarification and feedback to concerned members. In the case of ambiguous expectations, such clarification might take the form of more detailed job analyses in which the expected behaviors are clearly and unambiguously stated. When role conflict is evident, the conflicting expectations for a given position should be exposed. In some cases, it may prove possible to deal with such conflicts by changing the work requirements of a given position. This might involve shifting work and responsibility from a single position to several others or it might mean having to create a new position in the organization. In other circumstances, it may help if members simply become aware of the organizational "hot seats," those positions in which conflict is inevitable. Such awareness may be some help to the actor in the "hot seat" by giving him a basis for understanding the tension associated with his work. Moreover, awareness of the position difficulties may assist him in devising means for coping with what might be, in actuality, unresolvable conflicts. Furthermore, when all members are aware of the difficulties associated with certain positions, the chances of the actor achieving some degree of sympathetic compromise, rather than open hostility, from those performing reciprocal roles are increased.

We certainly do not mean to imply that verbal clarification will magically remove the difficulties associated with role ambiguities, role conflicts, inadequate role performance, and dysfunctional role reciprocal behavior. However, in seeking change in role-related behaviors, one should not overlook the possibility that at least some of the difficulties stem from participants' ignorance of the role factors involved. In any case, verbal clarification and feedback are obviously the least costly and simplest procedures available. Accordingly, one should certainly try them when conditions suggest that they are likely to produce some change or when other techniques are simply not feasible.

DIRECT ROLE TRAINING
FOR ADEQUATE PERFORMANCE

An actor may often fail to perform adequately in a given position simply because the component skills necessary for adequate performance are not present either in the actor himself or in his "reciprocal actors." In these cases, the expectations for behavior are quite clear and agreed upon by all participants. However, either the actor or his reciprocal actors may be simply unable to perform because of deficiencies in role relevant skills. These deficiencies may be task-intellectual or personal-emotional in nature. In either case, direct training in the component skills necessary for adequate performance is indicated. Direct training to overcome task-intellectual deficiencies is most easily understood and is commonly accepted as a part of training programs in most organizations. On the other hand, deficiencies in the personal-emotional skills so critical in social interactive behavior are not so readily understood or so directly dealt with. In many organizations, for example, it is expected that supervisors will routinely feed their evaluations back to subordinates. Yet it is rare that supervisors receive detailed training as to how feedback sessions should be conducted.

Many of the characteristics which we regard as making up the "personality" of the individual can be thought of as skills and trained in a direct fashion. Forceful-aggressive behavior, dependent behavior, sympathetic-nurturant behavior, empathy, and so forth, can be conceived of as skills much like any other and trained accordingly. In actuality, it is often precisely these personal-emotional skills which are critical in adequate role performance.

An example from the clinical practice of one of the authors is illustrative. A graduate student at a large American university had shown, for many years, extreme sensitivity to criticism. Several years of conventional psychotherapeutic treatment, though helpful in other ways, had not altered his excessive sensitivity. Negative criticism, even though very mild in nature, was the occasion for much self-doubting and even personality disintegration with crying and self-blaming. After several sessions, it became apparent that at least part of the student's difficulties stemmed from the fact that he seemed to have no direct way of coping with aggressive behavior directed at him. A role-playing situation was devised in which the student was trained in forceful-aggressive behavior in response to unwarranted negative criticism. The student performed detailed roles in which he responded aggressively to aggressive attack from the author. After several weeks, substantial changes in the student's behavior outside the role-playing situation became apparent and he later handled himself well in his oral examination, a situation which had previously caused him much concern and fear. In the case of this student, direct training in a personal-emotional skill resulted in improved role performance. He became more capable of meeting the expectations associated with the position of "graduate student." Moreover, this simple role-playing accomplished in several weeks that which several years of conventional psychotherapy had failed to accomplish.

THE ROLE-PLAYING SITUATION

There is no one way to conduct a role-playing situation. The problems to which the technique can be applied and the natures of the applications are limited only by our imaginations. Several important ingredients of the situation, however, can be specified.

Scenario

It is useful to have a sketch of a situation at hand at the beginning of the role-playing session. This sketch or scenario usually includes a specification of the roles to be played by the participants, their relationship to one another, and a brief statement of the situation in which the roles are to be acted out. A scenario for a role play in a management training setting might be as follows:

> Mr. Adams is a production manager for ATZ Dynamics. He has just been informed that it is necessary to lay off a quarter of his work force due to severe cutbacks in the industry at large. It is his responsibility to determine who will be laid off and the manner in which this will be carried out. He has called a meeting of his supervisors to discuss the situation and arrive at a proposal for action. Present at the meeting are Mr. Jones, Mr. Smith, and Mr. Frank. Each of these supervisors is determined that none of his men will be affected by the anticipated layoff.

Audience

It is useful to have an audience, which should not be passive, observe the role play as it unfolds. Aside from the learning that takes place through observation, the audience is a useful source of *feedback* to members of the role-playing situation. Its members can also be encouraged to participate directly in the role play in ways to be discussed below.

Role reversal

At various points in the role play, actors may be called upon to change roles, as when those occupying role reciprocal positions are called upon to assume the position of the central actor. In our scenario concerning layoffs in ATZ Dynamics, each of the supervisors might thus be asked to assume the position of their superior, Mr. Adams. Mr. Adams might, in turn, be asked to assume one of the role reciprocal positions. The purpose of the role reversal technique is to give the participants the perspective of the other person in the social interaction. It is often the case that awareness of the difficulties confronting the other person is heightened when one is required to assume his role.

Alter egos

It is often useful to aid actors in the role-playing situation by using audience members as alter egos. Alter egos may be called upon to enter actively into the role-playing situation in a number of ways. In some cases, they may be used to verbalize feelings the actor seems unwilling to express. Seated directly behind the actor, they may interject statements of feeling whenever they feel it appropriate. While the actor may be playing his role on a highly intellectual level, the alter ego may interject such statements as, "I feel hurt and disappointed," "I feel very angry with you," and "You frighten me."

Alter egos may be used to portray the behavior of the actor to himself. An audience member who gains a good feeling for the behavior of the actor as the role play unfolds may be called upon to assume the role of the actor and show him through actual enactment what his behavior looks like to others.

Finally, alter egos may be employed to demonstrate to the actor and role reciprocals that *alternative* ways of behaving are indeed possible. In the seeming turmoil of events, we often overlook the simple truth that a far larger pool of alternatives is available to us than we imagine. A deliberate search for and portrayal of such alternative ways of behaving is often an exciting realization that events are rarely frozen as we imagine them to be but capable of dynamic alteration as our behavior in relation to them changes.

Feedback

At some point in the process, the role-playing is interrupted so that both audience members and participants can comment on what has taken place. This feedback may involve the feelings aroused as well as perceptions of how the participants carried out their assigned roles. During the feedback session, analysis of the behavior of the participants can be extended to statements of how the situation might be handled differently.

Repetition of the role-playing situation

Following feedback, it is important to repeat the situation. This might be accomplished with the same or different actors. In any case, it is often valuable to attempt to act out the suggestions for change and alternatives arising from the feedback session.

PSYCHODRAMA

A more detailed and formalized approach to the role-playing situation is available in Moreno's psychodrama. While highly similar to the role-playing situation discussed above, Moreno's approach contains several interesting features worthy of mention. Let us consider the psychodrama briefly here.

Phases

The psychodrama begins with the person acting out situations from his everyday life. The scenes may be entirely realistic or consist largely of *fantasies*. This phase of the psychodrama is called the period of *realization*. In the second phase, the period of *replacement*, trained staff personnel assume the necessary role reciprocals either of real persons drawn from the actor's life or of those imagined in his fantasies. The final phase of the psychodrama is that of *clarification*, a period of analysis and feedback.

The psychodrama as envisioned by Moreno required a fairly large and well-trained staff. First of all, the psychodrama, like its counterpart the dramatic play, requires a director. The role of the director is quite active and he is expected to act as producer, social analyst, and therapist, though he is assisted by the trained auxiliary staff personnel necessary to help the actor carry out his role.

An interesting technique devised by Moreno is that of *soliloquy*. Following the completion of the action in the psychodrama, the participants are asked to reenact the scene as it happened but also to act out those feelings which they failed to express. These previously unverbalized feelings are spoken in a softer voice—in soliloquy.

ROLE PRESCRIPTION

A technique that we have derived from George Kelly's *fixed role therapy* (Kelly, 1955) is that of role prescription. Role prescription constitutes a practical way to arrive at mutually agreed-upon expectations for an actor's behavior. It involves collaborative effort on the part of an actor and significant others in devising and perfecting a role. When possible, persons directly concerned with the actor's everyday role performance should be drawn into the process. This not only increases the likelihood of a realistic appraisal of the role requirements but also involves others in a way likely to ensure future cooperation and commitment to the prescription devised for the actor. The following phases characterize the role prescription technique.

Construction of a provisional prescription

The actor and his role reciprocals meet in conference. The role reciprocals are given the task of operating as a panel of consultants to the actor. They are to assist him in arriving at a mutually satisfactory prescription for his behavior. Each is asked to begin by generating a list of the characteristics he would like to see in the actor in his performance in a given position in the organization. The actor, in effect, generates a list of statements which characterize himself as he would like to be. The panel of consultants does the same. The two lists then serve as a stimulus for discussion. Unrealistic expectations are discarded, compromises are arrived at between the actor and his role reciprocals, and so forth, until a provisional prescription is arrived at for the actor.

If one wishes, the same process can be repeated for the role reciprocals so that one ends up with two role prescriptions, one for the actor and one for his role reciprocals.

Rehearsal of the provisional prescription

Following construction of the prescription, a period of role-playing is conducted in which the actor attempts to perform the role as prescribed.

Analysis of role fit

The actor and panel of consultants then analyze how well the provisional prescription worked. The actor may comment on those aspects of the prescription that seemed awkward and uncomfortable for him. Role reciprocals may alter their expectations.

Modification of the provisional prescription

The period of analysis leads quite naturally to an attempt to construct another provisional prescription. The first prescription may be modified slightly or extensively as a consequence of experience with it. In any case, a second provisional prescription is constructed. A second cycle of rehearsal, analysis, and modification can be conducted. In fact, this process may be repeated a number of times until the actor and his role reciprocals are satisfied.

Empirical test of the prescription

The process of role prescription is incomplete without empirical assessment in the everyday life of the actor and his role reciprocals in the organization. Efforts are made to carry out the prescription as it has been finally revised and rehearsed in the role-playing situation.

Reanalysis of role fit

After some experience with the role prescription, the actor and his panel of role reciprocals again meet in conference to focus attention upon the viability of the role prescription. Decisions must be made concerning the inadequate aspects of role performance. It may be that the actor simply needs more experience with the prescription or even, perhaps, some training in role relevant skills. On the other hand, the problem may still be with the prescription and no amount of training and experience will correct matters. Or it may prove to be that all participants are satisfied with the prescription and its performance.

If appropriate, then, the prescription is modified further and training in role relevant skills for the participants is arranged. This cycle can be repeated as often as necessary—construction, rehearsal, analysis, modification, empirical test. While role prescription may seem a lengthy and tedious task, its rewards can be truly magnificent. Such deliberate effort on the part of the participants in a social structure to arrive at consensual expectations for behavior can surely minimize the problems of role conflict, role ambiguity, and role overload. Moreover, the collaborative aspects of the technique seem potentially fruitful in encouraging mutually supportive and understanding relationships between an actor and his role reciprocals. Each has had a hand in shaping the reciprocal expectations that are critical for adequate role performance and whose absence is often linked to dysfunctional role performances. Role prescription makes the optimistic assumption that, if effort and imagination are expended, an actor and his significant others may find equally satisfying ways of behaving. If actually realized in the organization, this would be a magnificent achievement, one well worth the admittedly high degree of effort involved.

SOME ORGANIZATIONAL APPLICATIONS OF ROLE THEORY

The foregoing discussion has attempted to outline some concepts from role theory and to describe some of the techniques which can be used by managers. In general, role theory applications—role-playing and role training—can be used in situations covered by the three basic categories of understanding and improving current relationships, trying on new roles, and handling future situations.

Understanding and improving current relationships

The techniques of role-playing and role training are useful in helping people understand and improve current relationships. Relationships between superiors and subordinates as well as the peer relationships among the members of a managerial or work team can be improved. Role-playing can lead to increased understanding of the particular events that lead to distortions, problems, and misunderstandings. In addition, alternative ways of resolving difficulties can be explored.

In supervisor-subordinate relationships, the supervisor may typically feel that the subordinate handles certain situations ineffectively or inappropriately. The subordinate, of course, may disagree. In normal discussion with one another, it may be very difficult for each party to understand clearly the motives, rationale, and behavior of the other. Each may not fully recognize the forces in the situation that led to the particular behavior of the other person. The role-playing technique can help by playing out the particular events which led to the conflict. With reactions and observations from observers of the role play, a fuller understanding by each party is possible. Alternative ways of dealing with the situation can be tried out directly by the parties involved or by other persons with the original actors now observing.

Another typical situation in superior-subordinate relations is one in which subordinates feel a lack of support from their supervisors. When specific situations can be identified in which that feeling is prominent, role-playing can be used as a way of understanding more fully the nature of the support the supervisor is not providing, why he acts the way he does, and what other acceptable alternatives are available. Other aspects of the role of the supervisor can also be explored with the role-playing method.

Members of work teams are often unclear about their own roles. They may also differ considerably with the way others in the team see their role. More clarity and specificity can be attained when people have an opportunity to act out situations in which role behavior is required. Opportunities for feedback and discussion are usually plentiful in this kind of role-playing situation and potential new agreements on the roles of team members are possible.

Role-playing can be a powerful instrument for looking at the

relationship between peer members or between superiors and subordinates on a team. It enables understanding of the roles each person plays
in specific situations around specific tasks by giving each person an
opportunity to explore and change, if he so desires, his role behavior.
A critical element in the effectiveness of this process is the degree of
trust and openness that people have about expressing themselves, both
as actors in the role-playing situation and as members of the audience.
Trust and openness are critical for audience members as well since re-
action and feedback are important factors in the process of redefining
roles and changing pertinent behavior.

Assuming new roles

Since organizational members may have little or no experience
on which to base new behavior, they may often find it difficult to assume
a new role. To understand the nature of a new role, the person must
have a chance to experience and learn the behaviors necessary to the
new role performance. Role-playing techniques are very valuable
in providing people with an opportunity to experience and explore
those behaviors. If, for example, a manager is required by a new managerial system to act in a more participative way, he may not really
understand what that means in terms of actual behavior. Role-playing
situations in which participative managerial behavior is tried and examined could be extremely helpful. As a further example, consider the
difficulties people have when they are asked to assume, without prior
experience, a leadership role which requires initiative and direction of
subordinates. It is difficult for them to know what this means operationally unless they have a chance to try out and experience initiating
and directing behavior and to understand the consequences that follow
from acting in these ways.

Handling future situations

Practice in dealing effectively with critical situations can be
accomplished with role-playing techniques. In this application events
can be examined prior to their occurrence and alternative ways of handling them can be tried and perfected. Meetings with customers or high-
level management meetings can be acted out in advance in preparation
for the kinds of issues that may be discussed or the difficulties that may

arise. One advantage, and an important one, afforded by this technique is that it enables the person to build a repertoire of possible behaviors. Not only can he generate and perfect alternative responses of his own, but feedback can further augment his repertoire. The opportunity to generate and utilize feedback from, and to try out alternatives suggested by, others with a different point of view is an asset of this method.

SUMMARY

In this chapter we have considered the important applications of role theory. We began with a brief discussion of role theory and the central concepts of position, norms, role performance, role reciprocals, role conflict, ambiguity, and overload. We discussed how a role analysis might be conducted and how the results of such an analysis might be utilized. We then showed how role training for adequate performance might be accomplished.

In addition to presenting the prototypical role-playing situation, we discussed two interesting variants, the psychodrama and role prescription techniques.

We considered direct organizational applications of techniques derived from role theory. We saw that in the organizational setting role-playing and role training can be used to understand and improve current relationships within and between given levels, assist people in assuming new roles, and aid in the handling of future situations.

In general, the usefulness of the techniques we have described depends largely upon management's willingness to use them, not only in training and development programs but as means to solve everyday problems arising out of the work situation itself. Most importantly, the success of these techniques is quite sensitive to the extent of development of trusting, open, and supportive relationships within the organization. They will not work well in contexts where significant amounts of distrust and suspicion are present and where a minimal amount of collaboration has not been achieved.

Finally, it is advisable in the initial use of role-playing methods to consider the involvement of a skilled third party who can assist with the structure and implementation of the methods as they apply to the specific situations which are to be examined. The manager who contemplates using these techniques in a continuing manner should of course acquire training in the use of them.

REFERENCES

Goffman, E. *The Presentation of Self in Everyday Life.* Doubleday, 1959.

Kelly, G. A. *Psychology of Personal Constructs,* Vol. 2. W. W. Norton, 1955.

Mann, L., and I. L. Janis. "A follow-up study of the long term effects of emotional role playing." *Journal of Personality and Social Psychology* 8 (1968): 339–42.

Moreno, J. L. *Psychodrama.* Beacon Press, 1946.

Changing Team Relationships

7

Today the team approach to getting the job done is becoming common practice in two ways. First, there is an increased awareness of the existence and function of "natural work teams," where "natural" means the people on the team are chosen on the basis of related jobs, activities, or functions as formally delineated by organization design. For example, one natural work team might consist of a boss (or superior) and those subordinates who report directly to him. Second, there is a rising use of temporary task teams who meet for limited periods of time and address their activities to limited problem areas. The growing complexity of organizational and technological problems has created a strong need for collaboration and coordination of the diverse resources which can be brought to bear on relevant problems.

Collaborative and coordinative approaches become critical when functions, tasks, and people are *interdependent,* that is, when the successful accomplishment of one function, task, or goal depends on how well other functions and tasks are performed. For a description of this sort of interdependence we might compare two teams, a football team and a track team. Although members on both teams are concerned with the team's total output they function differently. The football team's output depends synergistically on how well each player does his particular job in concert with his teammates. The quarterback's performance depends on the performance of his linemen and receivers, an end's on

99

how well the quarterback throws the ball, and so on. On the other hand, a track team's performance is determined largely by the mere addition of the performances of the individual members. Our discussion of teams and team development is concerned with situations analogous to the football team rather than the track team, situations in which organizational members are required to act in concert, and where each individual member's performance, as well as the total output, depends on the performance of his colleagues.

The study of groups has long been of interest to social scientists. Numerous studies of group behavior in a variety of settings have indicated the importance of group phenomena in American society and have led to increased understanding of industrial situations (Roethlisberger and Dickson, 1947), combat morale (Stouffer, et al., 1949), class status and mobility (Whyte, 1943), and communication behavior (Bavelas, 1951). Unfortunately, this apparent interest in groups of all sorts has not yet discovered the work team. Much more attention must be paid to the processes and effectiveness of work teams and to the development of methods and techniques for enhancing team operation. In this section several different perspectives on teams and team functioning are presented along with a description of what is commonly called team development.

THE TEAM AS A SOCIO-TECHNICAL UNIT

Task oriented teams may be viewed as two different, though related and interacting, systems. One is the social system and the other is the technical system; hence the team is essentially a socio-technical system designed to achieve certain specific work goals.

The nature of the social system

For purposes of description and analysis the social system of a work team is not unlike the social system of any group. This means that the dimensions of group social systems are applicable to work teams as well. The social system is comprised of two major dimensions, one being the character or *culture* of the group and the other being the *social structure* of the group.

The *culture* of the group refers to the shared set of beliefs, values, attitudes, and norms which guide and influence the behavior of members belonging to that group. Even in the case of temporary work teams, group culture, in the course of interaction over relevant tasks, soon establishes itself.

Group norms make the group's beliefs and values explicit and specify the mode of conduct along several pertinent group behavior dimensions. For example, group norms develop in the areas of the exchange of feedback on performance; the expression of feelings about individuals and group performance; the nature and quality of interaction; and the nature and degree of collaboration, participation in influence and leadership, and the resolution of conflict and differences. Norms, then, are a critical dimension which establishes and gives meaning to the character or culture of the group. The development of group norms is not as haphazard as it might initially sound, though. They are intimately related to the kinds of tasks that are required by the group, the nature and specificity of group goals, and the quality of leadership present in the group.

There have been numerous studies (e.g., Asch, 1951) and examples of how group norms influence individual behavior and guide group output. For example, the Western Electric researches (Roethlisberger and Dickson, 1947) point strongly to the effect of group norms around production and the power of their influence on group productivity. Norms help to identify and describe the group and provide definitions of acceptable behavior in specific situations. Acceptance of group norms correlates with the degree of cohesiveness of the group and hence can effectively contribute to the establishment of high coordination and motivation of team members. It must be noted, however, that group norms are shared by members because of the potential sanctions the group can invoke in the case of deviance. The ability of the group to apply group pressure or supply rewards in one way or another adds to the potential ability of the group to pool many resources for the accomplishment of specific group goals.

Social structure is the result of the patterns of relationships that develop among the members of a team. It may be influenced by the variety of roles represented in the team and the nature of required role relationships dictated by team goals and tasks. A number of factors contribute to the formation of the social structure of the team. One is the development of status and a status hierarchy, another may be the development of affective relationships among members. Although these are not unrelated the former may be contributed to by the occupational or positional roles of members within the organization proper while the latter is largely an interpersonal influence process.

By observing the frequency and nature of interactions—who talks to whom, about what, and how often—it is possible to chart the team structure and to identify the network of interpersonal and status clusters that exist. Structure is a clue to the potential attractiveness of the group and to the sources of influence within it.[1]

In summary, the structure of the team, together with its developing culture, comprises the social system of this particular work unit. The social system provides the potential power to act for or against those elements from the technical system which are essential to the accomplishment of team tasks.

The nature of the technical system.

In all teams there is, besides the social system, a technical system which concerns itself specifically with the organization and resources necessary for the accomplishment of its task. Some dimensions of the technical system are the organizational positions of members of the team, their technical specialties, often delineated by occupational roles, the necessary relationships among the technical specialties, the delineation and specification of tasks and assignments in relation to group goals, the methods and techniques employed by the team for the coordination of effort, the system of information generation and exchange, and the methods for identification and utilization of team resources. Together these elements comprise the technical system of the work team. This system influences the way in which members of the team collaborate by defining the relations among people. For example, positions of primacy in the flow of work and the physical positioning of people in relation to each other contribute to the development of status hierarchies, influence patterns, and interpersonal ties.

Although the technical system is a powerful influence on the social structure and culture of the team it is also influenced by the social system. The nature of interpersonal relations among team members and the development of group norms can be important determinants in the establishment and acceptance of work goals. The most important factor to be explored and understood in team functioning is *the interdependence of the social and technical systems*. For the manager to focus predominantly on one is to ignore the powerful influence of the other.

---

1. *Sociometry, a method developed by J. L. Moreno, is a technique for charting the structure of a group.*

SOME NOTIONS OF TEAM DEVELOPMENT

The development of a team is an educational process which, to be useful, must be an ongoing experience encompassing continuous review and evaluation of team processes and the identification and establishment of new and more effective modes of functioning. The concepts and techniques of team development are applicable to both old established teams and new and temporary ones.

The process of team development is not unlike the general change process formulated by Kurt Lewin (Lewin, 1958). The process uses a three-step procedure:

Unfreezing—the awareness and development of the need to change.

Moving—a diagnosis of the situation and the establishment of action elements.

Refreezing—the evaluation and stabilization of the change.

Initial activities in team development evolve around the unfreezing of old, well-established patterns of behavior. These patterns may be difficult to change in older, well-established teams, but consistent dissatisfactions with outputs are indications of the need to change. The team may feel that the way it functions could be improved and it may be motivated by the positive promise of increasing its output—in terms of both the task and the level of individual satisfaction. Even in new, temporary teams, members bring their own perceptions and expectations of what their behavior and that of the team should be like. Patterns of behavior are quickly established, often with little analysis of what the potential impact might be.

In the second step there is the identification of new and improved patterns of behavior and mechanisms for accomplishing the tasks of the team. These must then be realized in action before the last step, a freezing of these new patterns and an evaluation of how well they are working.

The real learning in this educational process lies not so much in the fact that the team has learned to do things in a different way, but more in that its members have learned to assess their own patterns of behavior, diagnose difficulties in those patterns, and establish new and more effective ways of functioning. Once this kind of learning process has been established (and it is never fully achieved) then a team can continue its development along the two significant dimensions of effectiveness and continued learning. The educational process is incorporated into the ongoing life of the group so that the team develops skill in the examination, diagnosis, and resolution of critical operational problems.

Viewing team movement: primary and secondary characteristics

Social scientists have been centrally concerned with studying and describing in general terms the quality of relationships among the members of a group. This concern is reflected by the often cited formulation by the sociologist Charles H. Cooley, who described the essential features of groups operating in either a *secondary mode* or a *primary mode* (Cooley, 1956).

In the secondary mode, group behavior has the characteristics of:

Impersonality • The members of the group are seen as resources in a particular task and as impersonally related to each other. Relationships within the group are primarily contractual and formal. They are designed for participation in group relations and for playing specific and designated roles in that relationship.

Limited participation • Individuals are limited to the specific specialties and resources which they are perceived as having brought to the group and to the task.

Intermittent contact • Usually group functioning is a series of tasks to be accomplished individually and autonomously. Periodic meetings are called for the purposes of updating and coordinating individual efforts formally, but the group members do not interact continuously.

In general, the behavior of individuals is best understood in terms of personal goals and personal contributions to tasks.

In the primary mode, group behavior is marked by:

Personal relationships • In addition to formal role relationships as designated by the group, personal ties develop.

Group cohesion • A degree of group solidarity develops in the sense that individual behavior can be at least partially understood from the point of view of group goals and aims.

Face-to-face interaction • A high incidence of face-to-face interaction occurs with the specific aims of collaborating on the total tasks, as well as on their parts.

Increased participation • Although there is the usual division of labor by specialty, the specific formal roles do not keep group members from sharing each other's tasks and goals.

The primary group mode is best characterized by a "we" orientation and an identification with group goals as well as individual goals. The secondary mode is much more of an "I" or individual orientation in which the formality of rules and regulations tends to guide the behavior and activities of the group more than the spontaneous interaction of the primary mode.

These characteristics and distinctions constitute "ideal types" and as such are abstractions of real life. Actual team relationships are apt to be a mixture of the two modes. The primary group concept in its extreme form can be detrimental to individuality and autonomy, while the secondary group concept, in its extreme, ignores the need for interdependent action and collaboration (Stone, 1969). As a general proposition then, teams must, to be effective, find the appropriate combination of secondary and primary characteristics. In general, however, team effectiveness is most enhanced when its pattern of behavior includes more primary characteristics than secondary characteristics. How much more depends on the situation and on the attributes of the team members.

One way of viewing team development, then, is to say that the group begins to move toward a pattern of behavior which incorporates more of the primary characteristics. The assumptions are that effective teams require more than merely setting a number of competent individuals to work on a very specific task and that there is a clear and explicit difference between *coaction* and *interaction* (coaction may be said to produce no more than the sum of the parts; interaction, a truly integrated and total view of the task and its outputs). Effective work teams do not just happen. Successful team efforts involve sharpening and fine-tuning the socio-technical system as by encouraging changes in the mix of primary/secondary characteristics.

Viewing team movement: task-process integration

Another kind of movement which occurs in team development is that from a polarized concept of task and process to one in which these components are seen as integrated parts of the total activity of the team.

The task elements in team activities are those things the team normally does in the course of its operation. "Task elements" refers to WHAT the team does; its productive output. For example, a managerial team may establish budgets, decide on alternative courses of action, and conduct employee evaluations. These things become the managerial WHATS; the things the team does as part of its charge and as part of its role.

If the team is a temporary proposal team, then the activities necessary for producing a proposal are the task elements: writing, drawing, discussions on technical aspects, etc.

"Process" refers to the HOW of the team. This means the team needs to be concerned about HOW it goes about doing and accomplishing task activities that are essential to its role and to its output. How do decisions get made, plans get established, and communication proceed between and among individuals on this team? How do the team members influence each other, how well do they use each other as resources, and how timely are their actions? These are the sorts of things that make up the processes of the team.

It is important in viewing teams and team development that the task-process dimensions be understood. Very often task and process are viewed as discrete entities. For example, although groups may set a specific time to look at process, it can be discussed apart from the context of the tasks and roles that are expected to be accomplished.

One view is that process analysis is unnecessary and that the business of work teams is work. The development of knowledge and concepts about organization has been in two separate traditions, that of scientific management and classical management theory and that of social science and human relations. Most managers, students, and theoreticians in this field may still view these traditions as separate from and even opposing, rather than complementing, one another. With this in mind, teams that persist with task activities when process analysis is required, inadvertently avoid change and improvement, though some groups may expend a good deal of energy in exploring, examining, and diagnosing process; this activity is an inadvertent avoidance of relevant and confounding task issues. What really is necessary is more of an integration of the two polarized components—task and process—of team activity.

Several decades ago gestalt psychology, an approach developed in Germany, established some useful concepts in the field of visual and perceptual structure. In general, the notion of perception as a predecessor to visual construction was an important thesis. One's visual field is constructed or organized into a gestalt or configuration of "figure" and "background." The "figure" is the focus of interest with "ground" being the context. The interplay between figure and ground is dynamic—different figures occupy different moments of attention and the details may command enough attention so that the remainder of the figure becomes part of the ground. The concept of the dynamic shifting of figure and ground can be useful in "visualizing" the dynamic interplay between task and process.

Task and process are viewed as being present together in any team, much like a gestalt configuration, so that the task and process elements must be dealt with separately as each becomes the figure or foreground and the other recedes into the background. Energy is wasted in organizations and teams when the task or process elements are the figure (foreground) and the team insists on pursuing those elements (either task or process) which are in the background.

SOME OPERATING PROBLEMS OF TEAMS

The problem of membership

Often groups must concern themselves with the degree to which people feel they are part of the team. The feelings and perceptions of members can contribute to or detract from the quality of an individual's contribution to team effort. Membership issues, if not resolved, may lead to the development of conflicting factions within the team and can hence undermine the overall purpose for which the team was formed.

The satisfaction of individual member needs

Attention must be given to the degree to which individuals derive satisfaction and personal accomplishment from their contributions. This dimension is often taken for granted and can inadvertently affect the way the group proceeds with its activities.

The tendency toward parochialism

One of the functions the team performs is to bring together diverse points of view and a variety of specialized skills. Because of this, problems may remain unresolved due to the tendency of individuals to view problems from their own particular perspectives. The opportunity to explore problems and approaches from many different sides can be lost in the belief that "our way is the only way." To ignore differences in perception and approach is to obscure a major determinant of creative problem-solving. The manager needs to be keenly aware of when differences change from resources to roadblocks.

Although specialization and expertise are important and should be preserved, it is equally important for team members to remain open to different perspectives, different points of view, and different approaches to the tasks before them.

The tendency toward losing differentiation

Team processes may inadvertently generate a conformity of ideas and approaches to the problem. Although group norms are essential in some areas and indeed can facilitate team functioning (like a norm around the open expression of feeling), teams that do not have the opportunity to generate differences continually face the danger of losing the zest, enthusiasm, and excitement of conflict and conflict resolution. While conformity in some areas helps maintain the attractiveness of the group to team members and provides some degree of satisfaction from social relationships within the team, it may also be the basis for producing a uniformity which can detract from the innovative and creative potential in the exchange among team members.

The task-process gestalt

Teams must be cautious about letting themselves be trapped into activity which is not pertinent to the pressing needs of the team. The pressures of time and other forces often dictate that the team persist with task activities even when analysis or change of the processes would be more appropriate. A team may also tend to persist in process exploration and the activity of diagnosing its operation even when further actions of this sort serve no useful purpose.

The problem of control

Early in team formation members become concerned about their influence and power. How can I exert some control over how this team operates? How can I influence others? they may ask themselves. When team members are doing what they want to do or have had ample opportunity to influence the direction of the group, the control problem becomes relatively simple. In developing teams, the strategies for dealing with control are fairly straightforward—procedures for maximizing influence are used and conflict resolution techniques are used. Unresolved control problems are usually indicated by excessive debate, argument, and outside manipulation aimed at persuasion.

GENERAL PROCEDURE FOR TEAM DEVELOPMENT MEETING

There is a generally accepted procedure for conducting a team development meeting. Although the specific content and activities of such meetings can vary considerably, the general format is probably applicable to most team development meetings. The procedure is more or less as follows:

Step 1: Initiating team development

Initially one or more team members might feel the need to hold operational activities in abeyance due to pressing problems in the way the team is functioning. This person could be the manager or team leader or any other member of the team. The decision to proceed with the team development meeting is usually a joint decision between the manager and the rest of the team. Although the manager could in theory make such a decision himself, the outcomes of a team development session depend largely on the degree to which members of the team are enthusiastic and motivated to engage positively and constructively in team development activities. A necessary element in the decision to proceed would be for the team to establish some broad objectives that they would like to see achieved as a result of the session. These objectives may be established by the manager or team leader or a subgroup. Again, to be operationally effective, such objectives should be agreed upon by the entire team prior to the meeting.

Step 2: Collecting the data

Very often information is collected from every member of the team prior to the meeting. A variety of methods or techniques can be used in this process (see Chapter 3), but it may be desirable at the outset to engage a skilled third party (an organizational consultant) to facilitate the planning and collection of data and to organize the information along dimensions that will be meaningful and relevant to the team.

Step 3: Planning the meeting

Once the data have been analyzed, even if this is done quickly and cursorily, the organizational consultant and the manager, perhaps with a few of the team members, can proceed to plan the meeting. They must determine the length of the meeting (which could be anywhere from one to four days), the specific activities that will occur, and the appropriate sequence of activities.

Step 4: Conducting the meeting

The meeting usually opens with a restatement and discussion of the objectives agreed upon and an exploration of the data collected with specific attention to the problems, issues, or general areas that the team wishes to spend its time on. The activities following this phase would depend on the number of people involved, the issues of highest priority to be dealt with, and the orientation of the manager and organizational consultant. For the most part, they should be designed to confront those issues which need to be discussed in order to produce effective problem-solving action.[2] It must be emphasized that the focus

2. For a survey of possible activities, see Fordyce and Weil, 1971.

for the meeting is to develop clear action plans for changing and improving the processes the team employs as it meets its work goals. In addition, follow-up activities should be planned at the close of the meeting. Follow-up should incorporate clear ideas for the evaluation of action plans, ways of exploring *if* and *how* the action plans have contributed to an improvement of the team's effectiveness.

Step 5: Follow-up and evaluation

At some later date, determined at the meeting, the team reconvenes to examine the degree to which action plans have been implemented, the difficulties encountered, and the support needed to implement the action plans effectively. At this point an evaluation may be made of how well the implemented action plans have contributed to the team's operation and new action plans or derivative plans may be developed from what has been learned so far. The action plans that seem to be working may be expanded and emphasized in the team's operation, while those that do not may be discarded.

In the sharing and interpretation of information, in the diagnosis of team problems, and in the development of new methods of operation, it must be borne in mind during a team development session that the elements of the team's socio-technical system do influence one another. The nature of the problems or issues explored and resolved in team development meetings may be related to either the social system or the technical system that comprise the team unit. The team must remain aware of the relationships between them and realize that solutions of problems in one area intimately affect the operations of the other.

ISSUES FOR THE MANAGER

The purpose of the above section has been to provide an overview of teams and team development. Team development meetings are designed to bring about important changes in the way the team accomplishes its work. For the manager who is presently considering or will consider team development activities as a method of change, there are several areas which he could weigh carefully. A team development effort cannot be thought of as a separate and discrete intervention but must be viewed in the context of a system of management which incorporates the values of participation, collaboration, and the maximum utilization of human resources. Within that context the following issues must be considered:

Do we have a team?

Team development activities are useful when members or activities of the team have some degree of interdependence, a term which refers to situations in which cooperation and collaboration are essential for the accomplishment of overall goals as well as of subparts of the task. The completion of any task or the achievement of any overall goal depends upon successfully completing other tasks and meeting other overall goals. When these essential characteristics are present, team action is appropriate. Managers may decide to engage in team development activities when little or no interdependence is present and when the managerial function is simply that of managing separate and unrelated functions. In this case team development sessions serve no real purpose, and since the context for such sessions is difficult to grasp, it is apt to create frustration and hostility among those who attend. The notion of organizational families, specifically a boss and those who report to him, as being analogous to a natural work team may be quite misleading. It is more fruitful for the manager to think carefully about the specific activities his subordinates engage in, the degree to which those activities are in fact interdependent, and the degree to which his primary job as a manager is the coordination of those activities.

Choice of third party

If it is decided to conduct a team development session, some attention should be given to the choice of a third party or organizational consultant. The manager should carefully consider the kind of consultant that would be most appropriate to the particular situation. For example, if many of the issues are in the technical system, a third party who has some knowledge of the type of organization, its clientele, and its environment may be desirable. It is also desirable to choose a third party who is perceived as being capable of facilitating the team development process, and whom the team, either by virtue of prior experience or through his reputation, feel is a trustworthy and competent professional. Although it is difficult for the consultant to be all things to all people, some preliminary consideration should be given to the types of problems that are likely to be subject matter for the session and the sets of skills a consultant should have to best facilitate their solution. Some questions for the manager are:

Does the consultant provide a different and stimulating perspective on our problems? One resource of the consultant can be his ability to help teams redefine and restate problems so that alternative viewpoints can arise.

Does the consultant have the ability to persist in difficult problem areas? His ability to maintain a confronting stance can act as a significantly educational model of behavior for the team.

Is the consultant able to lend support and encouragement? Most real changes in team operation will be difficult and sometimes painful transitional experiences. His ability to lend support and reinforcement will help the team incorporate their learning into behavioral change.

Does the consultant have "technical expertise"—conceptual knowledge, and the ability to apply it? A major resource of the consultant is his knowledge of team behavior, change processes, and facilitative techniques. His ability to apply this knowledge in the face of specific problem areas is a way of injecting new learning into the team's processes.

Purpose of the team building session

The manager should give some attention to whether or not a team development meeting is the appropriate change intervention for his situation, for pressing organizational problems can often be solved by other intervention techniques which are more appropriate to the situation. This can be done jointly with the manager, an organizational consultant, and other team members. Once the decision to conduct a team development meeting is made, however, and agreed upon by team members, it is useful to define its purposes or objectives. With an established purpose the thrust, activities, and outcomes enjoy a unity which may be lost if people attend such a meeting without a clear notion of what it is about. One of the critical success-failure factors of a team development session is the degree of frustration and anxiety that people are likely to bring to such a meeting. Although the acceptance of the purpose and objectives of the meeting will not totally dissipate such anxieties, the reduction of ambiguity and uncertainty around its purpose can be an important positive factor in the meeting's success.

Pre-meeting activities

Pre-meeting activities usually involve both the establishment of objectives for the meeting and a preliminary diagnosis via data collection and analysis of the team's operation. The manager must involve himself in the data collection plan to ensure that the information obtained is reasonably valid. He can do this by building into the data collection plan a wide range of data gathering methods and sources. In this way information obtained may be corroborated via other methods and may be examined from a variety of viewpoints. The time and effort devoted to this initial data collection may be well worth the expenditure.

Follow-up

Team development sessions can be a potentially potent vehicle for change. If such an intervention is successful the implications go beyond the team itself. The manager must remain alert to such questions as how the operation of his team affects other teams or suborganizations with whom it has relationships, how he and his team can seriously determine the impact of team development on the achievement of the team's work goals, and what additional resources are required to implement planned changes successfully. The more open the manager is to the exploration of these questions and the more he can face them from different perspectives, the more likely he is to deal with team development activities in the broader context of organizational change.

COMPARATIVE ANALYSIS OF THREE CASES

The following cases point out important differences and similarities in the ways in which team development sessions can be conducted as well as in their actual content. It is of value to consider these differences and similarities in some detail.

Case A

The manager of a large operational division suddenly found himself with four new members on his nine-member management team. Both he and his organizational consultant concluded that a team development session was needed to accomplish the following objectives:

1) To assimilate the four new members of the team;

2) To review "how things are going," and to see what new problems or administrative issues might be dealt with during the course of the meeting.

The meeting was discussed and scheduled in a regular staff meeting and its objectives were listed and discussed.

The organizational consultant interviewed all members of the team prior to the meeting, focusing specifically on the assimilation of new members—the roles of each new person as perceived by the old, the expectations of those roles held by the new incoming people, and, in particular, the expectations concerning those people with whom new members would have critical interfaces. In addition, the team members were asked for any other items or problems which they felt had high priority and needed working through.

The meeting began with the organizational consultant summarizing and feeding back the information obtained in the interviews. The data emphasized the expectations of each new person with regard to his role and how other people in the team saw those roles. The consultant also provided a summary list of additional issues about the team's operation that people felt needed some attention. This list included such things as more contact with the head of the division, a review of the budget procedure which people felt was bothersome, and problems in the personnel group and personnel evaluation procedures.

The meeting itself was designed in blocks of time devoted to specific activities. First, each new person had a chance to describe his individual role expectations, and to discuss them with the entire team while other members of the team were able to elaborate on their own expectations of that person's role. This activity continued with differences aired and elaborated until some reasonable agreement on the role definition for that individual was reached. Where agreement was not reached, the team suggested a plan for continuing to work toward agreement and the parties concerned committed themselves to it.

The second block of time was devoted to meetings of each new person with those few individuals with whom he had the most critical interfaces. During the third block, the entire group dealt with issues in which all of them were involved. For example, the revision of the process of budget establishment was one which everyone was involved and interested in and felt was a critical problem to be resolved.

This team development meeting was a two-day session in which the role expectations of the new members were dealt with in depth and where several other issues important to the team's operation were explored by the entire team. The assimilation of new members was clearly the issue of highest priority since the four new members could not contribute fully to the solution of other team issues until they felt at least somewhat secure in their team membership.

Case B

The Wage and Salary Administration staff group of a large organization found itself less and less able to meet the growing demands for its services. An organizational consultant was brought in to determine what problems and issues existed in the group and to provide some basis for understanding the forces which were contributing to its lack of effectiveness. After several lengthy group discussions the major determinants, as concluded by the consultant and agreed upon by the team, were:

1) The accumulation of interpersonal animosities and friction in the group.

2) The inability of the group to deal constructively and effectively with interpersonal conflicts over approaches to various projects assigned to the group.

3) The inability of the group to deal effectively with the role of the team leader and his approach to managing the team.

Interviews were conducted with each team member to further explore these issues. The interview data provided a clear picture of the network of those specific dyadic interpersonal relationships that were troublesome and needed resolution. In the words of some writers in this field, "There was a necessity for this team to heave out much of the garbage before they could effectively examine their work goals and methods of operation."

For the most part the team development session was spent in working through each set of interpersonal relations in which there were difficulties. The group, with some help from the organizational consultant, was able to learn both how to handle interpersonal difficulties and how to work toward conflict resolution more effectively. A major input from the consultant involved presentation of concepts concerning interpersonal relations as well as some practice in dealing with interpersonal difficulties.

An important part of the learning of this team, in addition to moving to a more sound footing in their working relationships, was some skill building in the interpersonal area so that potentially the group would never again get as bogged down as it was.

Case C

A group of theology interns were required, as part of their program, to team up with a group of older, established, ordained ministers to plan year-long projects in which they would work. They decided to begin the year by holding in abeyance the specific task of project formulation and project assignment, and to explore with one another who they were, what kinds of skills and resources they were bringing to the team, what kinds of roles and relationships might exist or develop, and how the team would make decisions about task activities and task related issues. They also shared their expectations about the kinds of things to which they would be willing to commit themselves during the year and the kinds of things they personally were hoping to get out of the year's work together. They were also able to discuss their own fears and anxieties about the forthcoming year.

Although objectives were established for this session, no data collection, in a formal sense, preceded the team meeting. The consultant was used primarily to facilitate the process and to make some suggestions for activities during the meeting which could resolve difficulties as they came up. The design of the meeting was general and the details were generated spontaneously as issues developed.

This instance is a case of a new team in the process of formation. Instead of exploring already existing behavioral patterns and diagnosing the way the team functioned, they spent a good deal of their time simply finding out who they were, the kinds and range of resources present, and making some preliminary decisions on the ways in which the team would function as it proceeded with its task.

Some differences

These are several of the more important ways in which the cases differ.

New team formation versus established team diagnosis • In case C, members met as a team for the first time. Although the purpose of the team was understood by all prior to the meeting, no real operating process had been established and very little information was shared about the skills and interests of the members of the team. The team development session in this instance was designed to begin a process of generating that information and to make tentative decisions about operating procedures. Case A is an example of a partially new team coming into existence. About a third of this management team was new, and disagreements around the way in which roles were to be played by new members were striking. Although other "team" issues were also part of the agenda, the major purpose of this session was the assimilation of new members. Case B is a description of a session involving an established team engaging in a process of assessment and resolution of operating difficulties. The three examples are slightly different, representing team development at various stages of a team's life.

Data collection on pertinent issues • In cases A and B information on relevant operating problems was collected and categorized prior to the session. In case C the agenda was generated as a first step in the session itself. In the first two examples a third party (organizational consultant) performed the function of data collection by interview and presented a synthesis of the information to the team at the start of the session. In case C the group generated the discussion topics and agreed to the order of discussion. The consultant merely facilitated the group interaction and communication processes so that the task was accomplished in the most expeditious manner.

Structure of meetings • The degree of structure which characterized each of the sessions varied. In case A, the design of the session, with respect to the ordering of the agenda and how much time was allocated to each agenda item, was carefully organized. The roles of new members were dealt with first, while other team issues were held in abeyance and allocated less time. The sequence and allocation of time reflected the priority of issues. Case C represents the antithesis of case A. The agenda was established by the team and the structure was dependent on the issue to be discussed. Since the team viewed this session as only a first step, no urgency existed to complete all agenda items; the team worked on each item until its members felt it had been resolved reasonably well.

Technical versus social issues • Team development sessions vary in their content. Although they invariably focus on the operational processes of the team, some teams discover problem areas in the technical subsystem while others find them in the social subsystem. In case A the areas of discussion for the team were primarily technical; they involved establishment of task roles and relationships, an exploration of budget formation, and personnel evaluation procedures. In contrast, case B presented an example where a team's operating problems were primarily social, that is, in the interpersonal relationships of its members. Can these be separated that distinctly? The obvious answer is no. As pointed out earlier, the technical and social subsystems affect each other considerably. These distinctions are helpful, however, as a means of providing a diagnostic springboard to the assessment of the team's operations.

Some similarities

There are some things that the three examples have in common:

Communication of objectives • In all cases the team members participated in the establishment of the objectives or purpose of the team development session. Care was taken in all cases to communicate the purpose of the team development session and to provide some opportunity for a discussion of the objectives of the meeting.

Interdependence • In all three cases some degree of interdependence among members characterized the team. Case A is an example of a managerial team, each member providing an important managerial function for the divisions. Case B is more nearly like the team whose members each bring a different skill to the performance of a particular function. It was only when these skills were integrated and made complementary to each other that the function could be effectively performed. In case C the interdependence rested on the resources each member brought to bear on the accomplishment of both project goals and the personal learning goals of the interns.

Process analysis focus • The team development session in each example was devoted to an analysis of *how* the team accomplished its task goals rather than on a "business as usual" agenda. Each session was representative of a "stop action" activity which characterized team development. All cases exemplify an explicit commitment to the diagnosis and improvement of operating processes.

Openness and willingness of the manager • The success of a team development session depends on the manager's openness and his willingness to engage in the process. In each case the manager or designated team leader demonstrated his commitment to a team development activity and opened up for review his own managerial approach. Particularly in cases A and B was time explicitly devoted to the influence of the team leader on team processes.

Primary and secondary characteristics • In all cases the team development activity can be characterized as having moved the group toward more primary characteristics, i.e., face-to-face interaction, increased awareness of the nature of the interdependence present, a sense of group cohesion and mutually held goals, and increased personal rather than formal ties. The very fact of the teams engaging in a successful team development process ensured this occurrence.

SUMMARY

In this chapter we have tried to describe the nature of organizational teams from the point of view of the interdependence of functions, tasks, and people. Teams have been presented as interdependent groups that function as socio-technical systems. Team development was conceptualized as an educational process in which the team learns to assess and move to the appropriate mix of primary and secondary characteristics. Team development not only refers to how well the team may be functioning but also to how well it is able to assess that functioning in an ongoing way. Some obstacles to arriving at that state were discussed briefly and a general procedure for conducting a team development session was presented.

Several case examples were provided as illustrations of the application of the general procedure. These served as illustrations of both the process and the content of several team development sessions.

The most significant thing for the manager to capture is probably the spirit in which team development sessions are conducted. When such meetings are conducted with positive and constructive intent they are almost always of benefit. When they are held in a critical and judgmental climate, resistance and defensiveness on the part of those present can be fairly well predicted.

REFERENCES

Asch, S. E. "Effects of group pressure upon the modification and distortion of judgements." In *Groups, Leadership, and Men.* Harold Guetzkow, ed. Carnegie Press, 1951.

Bavelas, A. "Communication patterns in task oriented groups." In *The Policy Sciences.* H. Laswell and D. Lerner, eds. Stanford University Press, 1951.

Cooley, C. H. *Social Organization* and *Human Nature and Social Order.* The Free Press, 1956.

Fordyce, J. K., and R. Weil. *Managing With People.* Addison-Wesley, 1971.

Lewin, K. "Group decision and social change." In *Readings in Social Psychology.* E. E. Maccoby, T. N. Newcomb, and E. L. Hartley, eds. Holt, Rinehart & Winston, 1958.

Roethlisberger, F. S., and W. J. Dickson. *Management and the Worker.* Harvard University Press, 1947.

Stone, Anthony R. "The interdisciplinary research team." *JABS* 5(1969): 3.

Stouffer, S. A., et al. *The American Soldier: Studies in Social Psychology in World War II.* Princeton University Press, 1949.

Whyte, William F. *Street Corner Society.* University of Chicago Press, 1943.

Changing Intergroup Relations

8

One of the most critical areas in any organization is that of dealing with relationships between two or more interdependent groups. It is often the case that effective task accomplishment requires the collaboration of several groups within an organization. Intergroup relations can be the most troublesome aspect of the organization's processes or they can be the most powerful stimulus for precipitating action.

The important dimension of intergroup relations is interdependence. That is, the accomplishment of the goals of each group depends on the actions of other groups, and, in part, on the degree to which other groups are able to achieve their goals. The completion of the tasks of each group separately contributes to the completion of the whole task. The individual tasks are meaningless, however, unless the integration or interdependence of tasks is explicitly recognized. For example, a production department's output is only useful to the extent that the marketing of those products is successful. Although the production and sales forces set separate goals for themselves, the success of each of the groups depends on the successful actions of the other. A more pointed example is the case in which several technical groups are required to contribute to the product contracted for by the company. The mechanical group must integrate its product with the electrical group, the electrical with the hydraulic or power systems group, and so on. It is often true that subgroups within a specialty must collaborate to complete a task successfully.

Realistic competition and open conflict are not necessarily detrimental to organizational behavior. The problems begin when distortions arise that affect the attitudes and behavior of group members in relation to those of some other group. Groups do and must conflict over the distribution of resources; the distribution of information, wealth, power, and status may produce discrepancies which in turn lead to conflict. Groups can, however, learn that conflicts can be settled in productive rather than destructive ways. Processes that move toward rational and creative ways of resolving differences can make the most of conflictual situations.

MANAGEMENT APPROACHES TO INTERGROUP CONFLICTS

Management has traditionally employed a variety of approaches to intergroup conflict (Blake, 1959):

1) *Separation.* This strategy rests on the notion that the conflict between the groups can be minimized if the contact between them is minimized.

2) *Affiliation.* In this approach the assumption is that if the two (or more) groups are united into one the conflict is likely to dissipate.

3) *Annihilation.* In this strategy management employs the notion that conflict is best settled when the groups "go at it"; the more powerful group will prevail and rightly so.

4) *Regulation.* Management establishes strong sanctions and legal procedures for dealing with intergroup conflicts.

5) *Interaction.* This approach seeks to resolve the conflict through discussion while maintaining the identity of each group and the functional relationship between them.

Most managers would probably agree that the first four approaches are less than optimal solutions. The fifth approach seems to hold more long-range promise of facilitating the creative and nondestructive use of intergroup conflict. For the manager it is likely to be the most difficult approach. It requires a certain degree of fortitude to maintain open channels of communication in the face of aggressive and often hostile group behavior. The groups will attempt to out-rationalize, out-explain, and out-manipulate each other in efforts to gain an advantage. Turning win-lose situations into potential win-win ones is a challenge in managing intergroup disputes.

Human relationships are generally not without misunderstandings and difficulty. The working relationships among groups are no exception. The "normal" routine and smoothly operating group machinery may run into blocks and obstacles that detract from the completion of tasks and the effective realization of goals. In the extreme, open conflicts may and often do arise between groups. Deep conflicts are often rooted in the *relationship*, although they often begin over differences on *substantive* issues. Their negative consequences may be listed as follows:

1) *Duplication of effort.* There are instances where groups duplicate the services or resources of others rather than confront the difficulties in the relationship. From an organizational standpoint this can significantly affect the utilization and allocation of resources.

2) *Sabotage.* One result of poor relationships is that each group may perceive the accomplishment of its own objectives in terms of how well it can impede the goal attainment of another group.

3) *Poor coordination.* When interdependence is a factor poor working relationships can influence the coordinative processes between the two groups and seriously affect the quality of the output.

4) *Inefficiencies of operation.* Very often slowdowns, schedule slips, and errors are products of intergroup disputes.

5) *Poor use of available energy.* Intergroup problems tend to consume time and energy. Groups must engage in coping activities rather than in relevant tasks.

Organizations tend to be naive about the powerful impact intergroup relations can have on the ability of the organization to fulfill its mission. They are equally naive about the relative merits and techniques of trying to improve or maintain working relationships among groups. It is important to devote time and energy both to improving deteriorating group relations and to maintaining relatively healthy relationships. The methods may be similar although the time, energy, and emphasis may be quite different.

When we talk about changing the nature of intergroup relations, we mean changing the dysfunctional aspects of the working relationship to more functional ones. Managers can learn to initiate and conduct relational changing exercises and to use creatively methods that can affect the ways in which groups collaborate when such behavior is appropriate.

The impetus and responsibility for change rest with the managers of the groups involved. The effectiveness of any method for changing the character of relationships depends upon the willingness of the individual manager to risk and experiment with the processes for bringing about change. When such attitudes are present the method itself is almost incidental. The point is that the manager is truly an agent of change; his ability to instill confidence in his group and encourage their active participation in any technique or exercise will most assuredly affect the outcome of the change effort. When the individual groups are splintered and fragmented any method of changing intergroup relations is not likely to bring about change.

In this chapter a number of techniques or approaches are described which may be used to improve relationships between and among groups which are engaged in a common mission. These can be applied to relationships between two or more groups and are applicable to groups of the same or different organizations. The criterion for the use of any of these methods is that the groups are in an interdependent or quasi-interdependent relationship.

FACTORS THAT IMPEDE EFFECTIVE INTERGROUP RELATIONSHIPS

Intergroup relationships are difficult to change and become more so as the relationship deteriorates. There are a number of reasons why members try to maintain the relationships as they are when even the most naive observer is aware of the inefficiencies in the way the groups function vis-à-vis each other. These are as follows:

Co-optation

Very often the possibility of being absorbed by "the other group" looms as an event to be warded off. These feelings can be real or imaginary; they nonetheless prevent any resolution of difficulties and create a strong motivation to maintain one's position and to engage in behavior that is aimed at avoiding co-optation. These activities can either look like attempts to discredit the other group or groups or to present a sharp and distorted view of the differences in function so as to make any collaboration, let alone combination, impossible.

The results of behavior directed at avoiding co-optation are usually increased alienation of the groups involved, an increase in the cohesiveness of each individual group, and less and less use of the rational processes of problem-solving. Energy is often expended on building the group and testing loyalties rather than on the actual tasks to be accomplished. In the extreme, the fantasy of co-optation provides an escape or defense which keeps the group from openly confronting and dealing with the relational problem. The frustration and anxiety of the situation is directed outward rather than toward the felt anxiety of the difficulties in the relationship and the inability to cope with it.

Loss of identity

For some groups collaboration is seen as having the potential to interfere in or to change their present sense of identity. If a group's concept of itself excludes the possibility of change, then relationships with other groups are perceived as potentially threatening the identity of the group. Preoccupation with such a threat to group identity makes the group susceptible to "hidden motives and forces" which can shape the self-concept of the group. Identity in the sense used here is the unique set of characteristics which create a feeling and aura of distinctiveness among members of a group. It can refer in part to the particular functions performed by the group and the feelings group members have about their performance of that function. It refers to the particular set of beliefs about the group and a mutual sharing of those things that comprise the essential character of the group.

When those shared sets of characteristics are threatened, anxieties may beset the group and appropriate defences employed. Most of these are aimed at maintaining the present state of the relationship. The energy for such activities is enormous but leaves little residue for working at the tasks that need to be done. There are studies which indicate that when an essential belief held by a group and linked to its identity is threatened the group cohesiveness is increased substantially and group loyalty may be put to work to block any change in intergroup relationships.

Territorial rights

In some instances the groups involved in an intergroup dispute block resolution of the dispute because of the possibility of an invasion of what the group deems to be its territorial rights. This can involve a change in the nature of the relationship such that some of one group's functions may become part of the other group's domain. In a way each group's sense of importance and control is at stake. The relationships between individuals or groups can be thought of in terms of states of "balance" and "imbalance." Once the balance is upset, efforts to restore the relationship to harmonious interaction will only proceed if the parties involved feel confident that their essentiality or importance will not be at stake.

One way of visualizing the intergroup relationship is through the sociological concept—the Norm of Reciprocity. There is an element of social exchange between groups which contributes to the stability of the relationship. Stable and effective relationships exist when the transactions between groups are in balance. Difficulties arise in intergroup relationships over differences in the perceived balance of transactions. When one group violates the norm, there is created a breakdown in shared expectations, an exploitation of power, and a process of maintaining the current status of the relationship until the violating group can be brought back into balance and stability.

Usefulness of intergroup conflict

Another factor which impedes attempts at improving intergroup relationships is found in the degree of usefulness members of a group may find in maintaining difficult and troublesome relationships with other groups. Identifying an external "villain" is always a useful mechanism for increasing group solidarity. To blame others becomes both an explanation for the group's current distress and a way of relieving the tension surrounding the depressing state of the relationship. The reduction of tension is as much a goal, though implicit, as it is an explanation for what is happening.

From the leader's point of view, poor intergroup relationships may serve to consolidate his position of authority or influence. In dealing with the "others" he takes on a representative position which is the key to the group's existence. Hence he may have a vested interest in pursuing the "improvement" of the relationship indefinitely as a way of maintaining his own power and importance in the life of the group.

Still another possibility is the usefulness of a noncollaborative climate in establishing sole ownership of a particular function or activity. When groups are expected to cooperate in performing a task and territorial rights are at stake, one or both groups may in fact set out to prove that the function ought to rest with them since cooperation is impossible. In this case the group may find ways to disrupt any possibility of collaboration as continual evidence of its position and of the unwillingness of the other group to cooperate.

Fear of losing

Most groups are reluctant to engage in diagnostic and change exercises. The resistance is more often than not centered around the perception that any resolution of relational difficulties means that there has got to be a loser. Although it is true that in some intergroup conflict dilemmas there could be a loser, it seems that when this attitude is generalized to *all* conflict situations it precludes resolution through more even-handed means. The two basic approaches to intergroup relations have been the establishment of a power base to be manipulated to win-lose tactics and the attempts at over-emphasizing cooperative-collaborative climates through mutual trust and positive regard. The focus on problem-solving and what actually needs to be accomplished is often buried in both of these methods.

The fear of losing is a perception or attitude which gives rise to either of the two approaches above and which prohibits engagement over issues in the relationship in a problem-solving fashion. The power approach, for instance, is more often than not concerned with winning rather than with the substantive issues to be resolved. The cooperative-collaborative approach may result in little more than avoiding the tensions associated with open confrontation of the issues and painful diagnosis of factors impeding the resolution of issues. Fear of losing is a force which operates both as a factor against reaching resolution and as an element contributing to a dysfunctional mode of resolving the difficulties in the group relationship.

METHODS OF CHANGING
GROUP RELATIONSHIPS

There are a variety of techniques which can be used to improve the relationship between two or more groups (Fordyce and Weil, 1971; Sherif, 1958), but because of their limitations, their effectiveness depends upon the prevailing conditions. The techniques will be described and a summary will be presented which indicates the necessary conditions for their use. This summary, however, is meant only as a guideline and not as a strict set of rules to be followed.

Negotiation by group members

In this method representatives of each group meet to diagnose difficulties and to negotiate the best way to reduce tensions and come to agreement on the issues facing the groups. The role of the representative is crucial to this technique, for it works only to the extent to which he really represents his group. Representatives can easily lose sight of the major focus of the negotiations and act more or less on their own behalf. If negotiations begin and continue in a win-lose mode, then defeat of a representative could threaten his position within his own group. A danger is that each group entrusts its representative with a group position which can powerfully constrain him and his ability to try for new and innovative solutions. This is particularly true if his status or sociometric position in the group depends upon his "winning" the original position of the group. The representative is faced with conflicts between loyalty, logic, status, and solution.

Negotiations can be around substantive issues or around the difficulties the groups are experiencing in their working relations. Often it may be useful to have a third party present to facilitate the process and maintain open communication among the negotiators. The choice of a third party must be agreed upon by the groups involved so that his observations and interventions are treated as "objective" rather than as advocating one point of view or another.

Exchange of persons

When tensions exist between groups it can often be advantageous to exchange members on a limited basis. The basic idea is that communication on a person-to-person basis can lead to a greater understanding of the "other" group; its culture, its goals, and its problems. The selection of persons to participate in the exchangé is important. Those whose attitudes are highly negative are likely to retain highly negative attitudes which may even be reinforced by the experience. Persons whose attitudes are fairly positive are likely to retain them and they are more likely to work toward ways to improve the relationship. It seems that the most effective use of *exchange* as a method of resolving intergroup differences results from involving individuals who are essentially neutral. These persons are most susceptible to influence and change, and cross-exposure can lead to a more objective evaluation of the intergroup situation.

The exchange of individual members poses some problems, however. An individual is apt to resist communication with members of the other group if he feels that it may violate the expectations of the group he is affiliated with. Individual change along the lines of changing one's set image of the other group or changing the way one relates to its members is difficult without the anchor of a reference group.

The exchange of subgroups, rather than individuals, has much more promise as a method. First of all, persons are moved into the other group with the support of some members from their own group. Second, it makes individual change much easier when the change is reinforced by members of one's own group. And third, changes in the total group's attitude are more likely when attitudinal changes have already taken place in a significant subgroup rather than single individuals.

The exchange of subgroups, however, is a more difficult operation, especially when those involved are significant persons in their group. The issues of betrayal, loyalty, and affiliation must be resolved within the group before this method will succeed. Moreover, it becomes a difficult plan to implement when day-to-day operations depend on those persons who are seen as likely candidates for an exchange exercise.

This format was employed in a state-operated department concerned with the rehabilitation of delinquent juveniles. The administration and staff working with wards within the institutions run by the department were at odds with administration and staff responsible for the parole function. Intense conflicts continually developed between the two groups. An exchange program was designed in an effort to improve working relations between the groups. Groups of institution staff joined the parole organization for a limited time and parole agents were assigned to an institution. Although the initial program was designed for a trial period, its success influenced the establishment of the exchange program as a regular part of the organization's routine.

Intergroup building exercise

An effective technique for improving intergroup relations has been developed and experimented with for quite some time. Based on therapeutic conceptions that have been developed in dealing with difficult relationships between individuals, its unit of focus is the group rather than the individual. The level of analysis is the group relationship involving the attitudes, stereotypes, and perceptions each group has of the other. The rationale is that negative distortions of the relational dimensions can lead to dysfunctional behavior and ineffective task coordination.

In this method, meetings are held with the total group when possible and with a significant number of representatives from the groups involved when not. The purpose is to identify the causes of difficulties and to generate solutions which can be implemented and which will improve the working relations between the groups.

To begin with, each group is asked to list its perceptions of the other groups. This procedure can begin in private group discussions or as a prelude to the exercise. One way of facilitating this process is to ask each group to answer the question: "What things does the other group do that really bug you? or get in the way of your doing your job?" In addition each group is asked to make predictions about the lists of the other groups.

The groups are then asked to share their lists. Reactions and questions are responded to at length, though a ground rule limiting debate and argument helps avoid rationalizations and justifications, facilitates the process of getting the data out, and establishes a norm of *listening*, a critical factor in effecting change in the relationship. At this point, careful *differentiation* of the groups, their needs, and their perceptions is important. It often helps to have the groups meet separately to discuss discrepancies in perceptions and the quality of the differences between the groups.

Once differentiation has been achieved (to some satisfactory

degree) and the differences between and among the groups are clearly
and sharply delineated, the *integrating* process can begin. Subgroups are
now formed by drawing a few members from each of the original
groups. These mixed, or cross, groups then begin the diagnosis of
relational difficulties and begin identifying the alternatives to improved
relationships. The problem-solving phase is important so that the energy
generated in the early steps of the exercise is channeled into concrete
and productive planning aimed at eliminating the waste and tension
in the relationship. Action planning and follow-up activities are essential to the success of this technique.

Some major ingredients in this process are the utilization of an
effective consultant to keep the process moving and to help facilitate
the learning generated by the exercise, the willingness of the leaders of
the groups involved to participate in the exercise, and an awareness of
the kinds of behavior which could contribute to the success of such
meetings or which could produce little change as a result of the meetings. The fewer internal problems experienced by the groups the better.
When groups are fairly cohesive and their attention is not directed
to internal matters, the more likely they are to see the problems in
external relationships and the more able they are to deal realistically
with them.

This approach focuses first on dealing with the emotion-laden
negative attitudes and stereotypes which create hostility and impede
working relationships. The second phase, of formulating solutions to
working problems, can only be accomplished when the animosities between the groups are resolved.

Criss-cross panels

The use of criss-cross panels is a variation of the negotiation
method described earlier. This is simply a method of choosing representatives. Each group develops a list of nominees whom they consider
to be "qualified" to represent them. The basis for selection can be
determined beforehand by the leaders of the groups or by a third party.
Each group then selects from the other's list those individuals who will
be members of the panel or negotiating team. The effect, then, is that
the negotiators simultaneously represent both groups.

This method partially reduces the representative's fear of the status reduction which may occur if he is perceived as not strongly maintaining his group's position. The representatives can be relatively free from the hero/traitor dynamic which is often present in negotiating teams. In addition, it provides an identification with the total problem, or at least reduces the parochial orientation which binds and immobilizes many negotiations of this sort.

The subject matter of the panel can vary from substantive issues confronting the groups to more emotive issues which may lie at the core of their inability to work together effectively. This method is most useful in situations where the groups are not extremely hostile toward one another and where there is some history of successfully working through difficulties.

CONDITIONS FOR THE USE OF INTERGROUP METHODS

There are certain mediating conditions which the manager can use as guidelines in deciding on an appropriate method. It is possible that changing intergroup relations from less effective to more effective may require a number of iterations of the same technique, or a plan which includes a sequential application of a number of different methods. Although these techniques were presented as separate or discrete ways of improving intergroup relations, any variation or combination of these may well do the job. Judgment which takes account of unique situational factors is important in making decisions about what to do.

The following conditions may serve as guidelines for the manager's choice of a method:

Negotiation by members

To apply this method, it is necessary that:

1) Group members have the ability to deal effectively with conflict and to work it through to an acceptable resolution.

2) Representatives have been given the power to make tentative commitments for their groups.

3) There is a high degree of trust and support already existing among members within each group. (Negotiation is likely to fail unless each group is fairly cohesive and internal problems are not obstructing efforts to resolve intergroup disputes.)

4) Task requirements leave enough time to work through relational issues.

5) The issues are more *substantive* than *emotive* in nature.

Exchange of persons

In this method a good deal of time is required to plan the exchange adequately and to work out details of selection and assignment. It works best when:

1) There are persons whose technical competences overlap. (For example, exchange of persons in an intergroup between parents and teachers would be less useful than between two engineering groups required to collaborate on a task.)

2) The difficulties are not deeply rooted in hostility. (Otherwise, the persons exchanged are likely to reinforce their attitudes and stereotypes of the other group.)

3) Preliminary diagnosis of the situation indicates that difficulties are primarily due to lack of understanding and appreciation of each group by the other.

Criss-cross panels

This method is probably most effective when:

1) Relational difficulties are relatively minor.

2) The groups have some history and experience of working through relational difficulties.

3) There is a general willingness of the groups to work through problems and reach genuine solutions.

4) It is relatively easy to get both groups to commit themselves to solutions reached by the panel.

Intergroup building exercise

This method is most useful in situations where:

1) Deep relational problems are at issue and are seen by the managers as critical to their operation.

2) Key group leaders have expressed some willingness to address the emotive problems underlying difficulties in the relationship.

3) Both groups can agree on the choice of a third-party facilitator. (This method does work best when an objective third party is used to monitor the process.)

4) There is some prior agreement by the manager to utilize the outcomes of the exercise *and to follow up* on the actions developed by the group.

5) Adequate time for planning, preparation, and implementing the process can be set aside. (The intergroup building exercise involves a process of *differentiation* and *integration* and must be allowed to complete itself. Moving ahead too soon can result in emotive issues being only partially resolved and in a lack of enthusiasm for solving the more operationally oriented problems.)

ILLUSTRATIVE CASE

When management decided to split a very large engineering division's function into two subfunctions, the division was also split into two. A new head was appointed for the new division and he promptly proceeded to recruit from the original division the personnel necessary for the performance of his division's function. Although the general roles of each division were articulated and communicated by top management, the task areas which overlapped and needed to be coordinated could not be reliably predicted. The critical areas in the role definitions had to await actual task experience to be seen clearly.

As the new division grew, however, there arose increasingly numerous conflicts over the decision prerogatives of each of the two divisions and over the allocation of resources. Strong differences in opinion over the primacy of each division's function as it related to the overall mission of the organization emerged.

The pressures of day-to-day activities contributed to the growing delays that seemed to prohibit management from dealing directly with the increasing factionalization and friction. The hostility between the two division heads seemed to permeate their respective organizations. When the difficulties between the two divisions began to affect other parts of the organization, top management was finally prompted into acting. With the help of an organizational consultant, it was decided to develop a program which would explore and resolve the relevant issues prohibiting effective coordination and collaboration between the two groups.

After several exploratory interviews with each division head a planning meeting was conducted. The two division heads in conjunction with the organizational consultant agreed that some form of intergroup development exercise would be an appropriate approach to alleviating some of the problems and issues confronting the two divisions. The exercise proceeded in two phases:

Phase 1

Several sessions involving a number of representatives from each division were held. The representatives were identified by the head of each division as individuals who were seen as key figures in influencing the direction that each division was going. Each divisional meeting was held separately in preparation for a joint meeting of representatives. At that session each division shared difficulties and their preliminary diagnosis of the causes for such problems.

Phase 2

With this as a backdrop, the representatives, with help from the consultant, planned the exercise.

A larger meeting was held which included all the management personnel from both divisions. The format for this meeting followed the format used in the meeting of representatives. Each divisional management independently identified the nature of the difficulties which they felt existed. Those difficulties were next shared and discussed with the entire group. Smaller subgroups of people from both divisions then determined which of the problems needed to be resolved.

The issues that emerged were needs for:

1) A more explicit allocation of resources to each division.

2) Clearer definitions of decision areas directly related to customers and contracts.

3) Establishment of procedures for increasing the degree of coordination on activities which involve members from both divisions.

Task groups made up of members from both divisions were assigned to develop solutions to these areas and to present their recommendations to the management groups of both divisions.

Communication between the management people and the working level was strongly encouraged and proceeded as the intergroup meetings and task group products emerged. Opportunity for cross communication at the working level between the two divisions was also initiated by the task groups in an effort to generate ideas for the solutions of problems. The task groups reported back one month later. From their recommendations and ideas for solutions the group was able to make modifications and agree upon a plan for approaching each of the original problem areas. These solutions were then implemented.

Four months after the implementation of the solutions the original management group met again to assess the degree to which group relationships were improved and to discover what new issues, if any, had developed. Several new task groups were formed to continue the work on improving divisional relationships. It was evident to both groups that they had found a mechanism for confronting inevitable relational issues. Moreover they could now deal with those issues in a much more expedient and efficient way.

SUMMARY

Approaches to resolving intergroup conflicts tend to fall into one of three categories, either moving the groups away from one another, moving the groups against one another, or moving the groups toward one another. Methods which fall into the first two categories tend to be temporary in nature and have very little learning impact. In addition, they may produce residual effects which are worse than the original conflict. The manager should carefully weigh the implications of resolving any intergroup disputes by employing such methods. Although solutions which fall into the first two categories may seem expedient and relatively easy to implement, the decision to use them can have profound and pervasive effects on the organization and its processes.

The area of intergroup relations and the ways in which the organization legitimizes dealing with and coping with conflicts can significantly influence the organization's culture in general. It can be a culture which deals openly and directly with the issues, managing differences and conflicts creatively, or it can suppress the open expression of feelings and difficulties and deal with its problems in procedural and restricted ways which limit creativity in problem solutions.

REFERENCES

Blake, Robert R. "Psychology and the crisis of statesmanship." *The American Psychologist* 14 (1959): 87–94.

Fordyce, J., and R. Weil. *Managing With People*. Addison-Wesley, 1971.

Sherif, Muzafer. "Superordinate goals in the reduction of intergroup conflict." *American Journal of Sociology* 63 (January 1958): 67–85.

The Use of Internal Consulting Teams

9

The techniques described in the preceding chapters were developed in part from the creative application of the principles of behavioral science to the process of organizational change. A few of these principles have to do with the *consultative process* and the use of consultants in change efforts. Most organizations that feel the need for change and decide to try to improve their effectiveness make some use of an objective third party—the organizational consultant—who is usually from outside the organization.

THE CONSULTATIVE PROCESS

The concept of "consultation" has many meanings. In this book, it is used in a general way to mean an activity performed by one person in relation to another to help him apply the resources necessary for solving a problem. This definition assumes that the consultant-client relationship is voluntary and that both client and consultant desire a solution to the problem. The client can be viewed as either an individual in the organization, a suborganization like a work team, or the organizational system.

There have developed two primary traditions in organizational consulting. The first may be characterized as an approach which provides *technical* service to the client system. The second is essentially a systems approach and regards consultation as an *organizational process*.

Under the first approach, a consultant is called in to help when an organization experiences a problem with which it is unable to cope. Within reason, he usually takes the statement and description of the problem at face value and spends most of his time in applying the special techniques at his command. His major concern is finding an adequate solution to the problem. Once this is accomplished, his job is essentially done. This viewpoint is analogous to Eliot Jacques' description of the "technocratic approach" to dealing with social problems, in which the consultant does things *to* people rather than *with* people (Jacques, 1947).

Under the second, the consultant is basically oriented toward diagnosing the organization's ability to cope with problems. His intention is to facilitate the development of a climate in which problem-solving resources can be identified and developed. His activities are often concerned with helping the organization build and incorporate the skills necessary for an ongoing assessment of its problem-solving capability and for continually strengthening those areas in which improved problem-solving is necessary.

The advantages of the *technical* tradition are that the expert brings to bear a knowledge and skill that the organization may not require on a continuing basis, and that he can attack the problem in an expedient manner. The problems with it involve the danger of an emerging dependence in the client-consultant relationship in which the responsibility for coping with difficult situations is always shunted off to a consultant, and the near certainty that new roles and new skills will not be developed by the people in the organization.

The *organizational process* approach keeps the responsibility for change squarely with the client while focusing on the client's own problem-solving ability. It stresses a joint diagnosis of the situation and a collaborative approach to the problem. It is an approach, however, that can be applied too often. There are occasions when simple technical solutions are appropriate and where emphasis on "process" may be unnecessary.

Both traditions can play an important role in organizational change. They represent in action the task-process dichotomy so prevalent in approaches to change and so often viewed as *opposing* approaches rather than as available alternatives or complementary viewpoints. The organizational consultant may find it necessary to function in a number of different modes depending on the needs and requirements of the client system.

ROLE OF THE ORGANIZATIONAL CONSULTANT

By viewing the consultant as providing a mix of task and process inputs to the organization, a variety of possible third party roles may be conceived. Regardless of the mix, however, there are several dimensions of the consultant's behavior common to any approach. His efforts are aimed at:

1) Facilitating the diagnosis of the problems, difficulties, and issues that indicate the need for change. He may do this by providing some expertise in a particular technical area or by suggesting ways to encourage organizational diagnosis.

2) Assisting the clear statement and communication of what is intended by and expected from the change.

3) Pointing out those things which are not seen or not easily said by the members of the organization. He acts as a mirror, reflecting the total picture of the moment. Being outside the immediate situation, the third party may see things in a different perspective or see things which are less than obvious to those directly and emotionally involved in the change effort.

4) Facilitating the formulation of a change plan. Once change goals have been established and accepted, the third party can help in the formulation of specific plans for implementing change. Change, to be effective, cannot happen haphazardly; action components, time elements, and sequencing of events must be considered, thought through, and planned. The consultant can point to places where plans are necessary and where planning must be sharpened.

5) Acting as an integrator. A variety of activities and difficulties may be involved in planning and implementing change. The third party can bring together those individuals and groups within the organization whose efforts need to be coordinated, and he can act to resolve the difficulties, even to forecast and forestall potential conflicts.

6) Providing initial continuity. The third party can provide substantial follow-up to the beginnings of a change effort. He can play the role of gate-keeper and communicator and keep the schedule of events flowing.

INTERNAL CONSULTING TEAM MODEL [1]

Only a truly versatile and flexible individual can apply all the various resources required for an effective organizational change effort. Hence, there are occasions when situational factors make it necessary to employ a different organizational consulting model. For example, when time and priorities indicate that the organization requires extensive consulting resources to be applied in a concerted way, in a relatively short time, the use of an "external" consultant may be neither the most feasible nor the most effective approach.

The consulting resources within the structure of most organizations are not developed or utilized or, usually, even recognized. "Internal" consulting help has far more potential than most organizations realize. The decision to expend energy, time, and money in developing individuals with the understanding and skill to provide organizational consulting help internally is often a difficult one to make. For one thing, it means a redefinition of most managerial roles to include a consultative function. It also means a change in the traditional concepts of the "consultant" role, for consultative help can be adequately provided from *internal,* as well as *external,* sources.

The model described herein suggests a number of distinct but *overlapping* phases that describe and facilitate the developing consulting team and its developing consultant-client relationship (Table 1).

The major activities of the consulting team are listed according to the sequence of phases of the change effort. The phases follow the model described in much of the literature on organizational change (e.g., Lippitt, et al., 1958). Basically, it involves the steps of (I) preliminary problem identification, (II) data generation and diagnosis, and (III) action intervention as essential elements in the process of change. As the change process progresses and as the team develops, particular activities assume major importance. For example, although some team formation activity may take place during Phases II and III the team formation activity has its major emphasis during Phase I.

A theoretical model has been developed describing a continuum of "consulting styles" or modes and the relationship of those modes to an organizational change process (Margulies and Raia, 1968). The model schematized the consultant role as that of expert at one end of the continuum and that of clinician at the other end. Its major point

1. *This material was liberally borrowed from Margulies, 1971.*

TABLE 1   Description of Activities of Consulting Team

	PHASE I	PHASE II	PHASE III
Consulting Team Activities Related to Its Own Functioning	Team Formation—assignment of tasks, decisions on how to proceed, how the teams will function together.	Consulting team development—identifying team resources, planning the use of resources.	Review and evaluate activities, review problem priorities, decisions on development of consulting resources.
Consulting Team Activities Related to the Client	Preliminary data collection. Preliminary problem identification of system and subsystems.	Suborganization work—identifying department issues, problem-solving in departments. Coaching department managers. Planning ongoing organizational developments.	Total system diagnosis. Shifting responsibility of data, diagnosis, and intervention to client.
Summary of Major Activities	Team Formation Overall Data Pooling System Diagnosis (Preliminary)	Department Data Collection and Diagnosis. Action Interventions Relationships Among Departments	Review and Evaluation Total Organization Diagnosis. Shifts to Concerns About External Relationships

was that the interventional mode could and should vary along the continuum depending on current organizational and situational factors. Chronologically the consulting mode suggested in the model progresses from expert to clinician as the organization matures and as the organization moves toward more of a problem-solving approach to its own function. Phase I then, so far as the consulting team is concerned, seems to coincide with the expert end and Phase III with the clinical end.

The use of consulting teams can best be understood by means of a case example. The model in Table 1 may be used as a guide in following the sequence of activities of the team and the relationship of those activities to the change process. The descriptive material within each phase is organized according to the activities pertinent to the development of the consulting team and the activities of the team in relation to its client. The case can thus be understood from the point of view of the consulting team as well as from the point of view of the organizational change process.

ILLUSTRATIVE CASE

Organizations have become increasingly aware of a variety of problems with immediate or potential systemic impact. In the case presented here, one such problem involved the Management Systems Group of a large organization. The company had seen fit to allocate significant resources to this group since it played an important part in the company's planning and control function. For a variety of reasons the MS group was never quite able to fulfill its function or the potential expected of it. The group's image of itself as a "system creator or developer" had important behavioral consequences. Primarily, it created a serious schism in the group's relationships with other parts of the organization. This was particularly true with those groups that were expected to use its products but felt that they did not meet their day-to-day needs. The widening gap between "producer" and "user" simply perpetuated itself. The greater the animosity and hostility between MS and its customers, the more difficult it became for MS to deal with the friction and the easier it became for its members to believe in the inadequacies and incompetencies of the other groups. Of course, the more MS behavior reflected these beliefs, the more true they became. The relationship problem was clearly seen by many observers as the critical dimension in the success (or failure) of MS.

Internally the MS organization was composed of several functional groups and an internal service group. The functional departments each had responsibility for management information systems of a particular type. For example, one area concerned itself with material control systems, another with project management systems, another with financial systems, etc. The service department was responsible for providing training, consultative support, and maintaining technical expertise and knowledge of the state of the art. The necessary linkages among the functional departments did not seem to be well established, although they should have been. The service department, in its relationship to the functional departments of the MS group, enacted in microcosm the producer-user conflict that characterized the MS-customer relationship.

The internal difficulties resulted in lagging schedules and merely convinced the users of the inability of MS to perform, or worse, of its disconnectedness from the day-to-day problems of the organization.

In general then, the membership of MS had developed a defensive stance toward the user population and became more and more defensive as morale degenerated.

The MS group was seen by top management as providing an important and necessary function. The question thus became increasingly that of providing the help necessary to transform the MS from its current state into a more effective, fully functioning part of the organization.

An external consultant had suggested to the Personnel Manager and the MS Director the notion of an internal consulting team to provide additional resources during this critical period. When the concept was accepted, the three identified specific individuals in other parts of the company to link with each MS manager; they based their choices for the team on a combination of three factors, expertise, competence, and the probability of acceptance by the particular MS manager. The MS Personnel Manager talked with each of the individuals selected and interested them in joining in the experiment. This was the beginning of the development of the internal consulting team.

Phase I

Formation of the consulting team • Each of the selected individuals, in addition to his normal job assignment, became part of the consulting task force to provide the necessary "change" resources to MS. The skills within the team varied; in some cases, the expertise of the individual was more "technical" than "process" oriented.

The team's first task was to deploy its resources. Each member of the team was to initiate a consulting relationship with a departmental unit in MS; specifically, this meant a consultant to each functional area in the MS organization, as well as to the MS director and his managerial "team."

The newly formed consulting team began first to tackle the problem of its own development. Questions were raised and addressed around the need for coordination, sharing of information, agreement on general approach, and ways in which the members of the team could learn from one another. The general solution was for each consultant to make his own contract with the manager of his assigned functional area and begin in his own way to create the appropriate client-consultant relationship. Each one then collected data via interviews from his assigned functional area, specifically around the problems each department was experiencing.

Regular consulting team meetings were established as the operational mode of the team; team members were able to get help in resolving some of the problems they initially faced in their assigned functional areas. The problem of entry and acceptance was a critical one. Regardless of the mandate sanctioning the consulting team approach, the degree to which individual managers utilized the consultants depended largely on the degree of trust and competence the consultant was able to convey to the client. The general climate in MS made entry particularly difficult. The organization, more often than not, tended to see "outsiders" as meddlers and tended to see "expert" intrusion as a threat to the degree of control it could exercise over its own affairs.

Client-oriented activities • Most relationships began in a "coaching" mode, with the primary client the department manager. The greater the degree of trust between the consultant and the manager, the more the consultant was able to work with other segments of the department. As the consulting team became more and more involved with its clients, data collection became an important and natural part of the consultants' activities.

At this point, the content of consulting team meetings changed from team development to working sessions. The team members began to pool their organizational data and began a diagnosis of the problem areas in MS. This was a necessary step in coordinating the *separate consulting activities* into a *concerted effort*. Although the consulting team members were working primarily with their own clients, it was felt that there were overlapping and common issues and that the members of the team could help one another by sharing their data and jointly generating approaches to problems.

Phase II

Continued formation of the consulting team • From data sharing and joint diagnostic sessions each consultant was able to arrive at some action steps aimed at "working" those problems in his assigned functional area. Early in this phase strategies were directed at such internal problems as:

1) Managerial communication;
2) Coordination of activities;
3) Supervisory styles;
4) Definition of roles and mission;
5) Motivation and morale;
6) Technical competence.

In some instances, the action steps included further data gathering and a more detailed diagnosis of the problems.

The consultant then met with the management group to discuss the data and develop a strategy for beginning to work on the problems outlined. One such action was a two-day team building meeting with the entire suborganization and a series of management team meetings aimed at solving the problems identified above.

Consulting team meetings continued on a regular basis with continued pooling of information and updating of the consultants' interventions. This included a review of the problems previously identified, additions, deletions, and a review of the "remedial" interventions that had occurred or that were going on.

The MS organization was beginning to act more like an organization than like an aggregate of separate functions. One important action toward this end was a meeting of the top management of MS. The consultants played two important roles in preparation for this meeting:

1) They became data gatherers and diagnosticians to help focus this top team meeting on the perceived issues of MS.

2) They coached their own functional manager by dealing with anticipations, apprehensions, and expectations of the meeting.

The meeting seemed to have positive results. The MS internal interface problems were addressed and several key action steps were identified as a way of beginning the unifying and coordinating process that seemed so central to this organization. The managers agreed that continued efforts in this direction were worthwhile.

Client-oriented activities • Consulting team members continued their suborganizational focus and worked primarily on the internal organizational development of each functional area. More and more, however, the tenor of the consulting meetings seemed to drift toward concerns that represented total MS issues and especially toward those that were reflected in the relationships among the departments.

Phase III

Maturing client-consultant relationship • As concern focused on the total organization more and more, the consulting team made an explicit attempt to concentrate on the total organization rather than on the subparts. Most of the diagnosis focused on the overall MS "climate." For example, a good deal of information pointed to the separateness of the organizational elements and how that was related to the relationships among their managers. Unwillingness to share resources, a lack of openness about the current status of things in the functional areas, and unresolved conflict between MS and its users seemed to be the most prominent concerns. It is important, however, to note that although some of these problems were identified earlier, the readiness of the client system to deal with them was considerably different at this point in time than it was during Phases I and II. Only now could the consulting team meet productively with the MS Director to map out alternative strategies to deal with these overall problems, particularly those which were customer-related.

Several events seemed to mark a shift in the organization's health. One was the establishment of an organization-wide Training and Development Council composed of line managers. The Council had representation from all functional segments of the organization. A second indication was the participation of line managers in data collection and the diagnosis of MS organizational problems.

The consulting team reviewed the status of the problem areas and the action plans they had established during Phases I and II and a gradual updating of the inventory of problems took place with more and more inputs from line managers and the Training Council. In this phase the consulting team made an explicit effort to shift their activities to people in the MS organization. Line managers met with members of the consulting team periodically to learn about diagnostic techniques and strategy formulation. At the same time there began to develop an increased desire among line managers to use one another as consultants. The relationships among the functional areas and the MS climate in general had changed significantly. There was much more trust and collaboration than several months before.

As the organization began to take more responsibility for dealing with its internal problems and external relationships, the consulting team began a process of "phasing out." The organization had less need for the magnitude of organizational consulting help the team represented. The problem focus became oriented less toward MS and more toward improving relationships between MS and other relevant groups in the organization.

ISSUES IN THE USE OF INTERNAL CONSULTING TEAMS

There are times in an organization's life when concentrated resources are needed to implement change. It may not be feasible in some instances to muster external consulting resources to do what is required, especially over very short times. One very real issue in an internal consulting team effort is the willingness of the organization to release people from some of their day-to-day tasks to engage in consultative activities. Internal resources have the advantage of at least some knowledge of the organization, its culture, its dynamics, its goals, its objectives, and even, to some extent, the personalities involved within the suborganization in which they are going to be working. The time and energy required for any external consultant to acquire this kind of intimate knowledge of the organization make that alternative less than satisfactory. This does not mean that the external consultant cannot play any role in this process; not at all, but his role *is* a highly specialized one. He may, for example, act as a consultant to the consulting team, which, in a very real sense, faces the same problems around the utilization of *its* consulting resources as the organization of which it is a part.

Resistance to consulting help

Initial resistance to consultant intervention may stem from a global opposition to intrusion from outside parties and from a general resistance to change implied by the presence of consultants. The "sick stigma" which organizational members may attach to the acceptance of consulting help may be a factor to reckon with if the client-consultant relationship is to be fruitful. Even when organizations are promised resolution of difficulties, consultants may suggest new, different, and unfamiliar modes of operating which are seen as a threat to the stability of the current coping processes. In addition, when the trust level between client and consultant is low, the client may view consultant interventions with suspicion and doubt.

Resistance to the consulting team is compounded by the fact that the consultants are also members of the organization. Sharing information which the manager feels is private data becomes a major decision even under conditions of high trust. Resistance which occurs later on in a change program may have a rational base, for difficulties with the environment may constitute a legitimate resistive force which warrants discussion between client and consultant. In addition, the inability of the client system to assimilate or implement changes rapidly due to a lack of resources can be easily misinterpreted as resistance to consulting help.

Differentiation and integration

One important function of the consulting team is that of integrating or pulling together the separated (and often alienated) parts of the organization in which it is working. This can be accomplished in a number of different ways. The first, and perhaps the most obvious, is by acting as a switching center for information. This simply means that the consultant shares all data pertinent to the total organization (*not* privy data) with his client. Separateness and alienation among parts of the organization are partly due to a lack of information about other parts of the system. *This kind of function cannot, however, be continually performed by the consulting team.* There must be a time in the growth process of the organization in which it in some way takes on the responsibility of data collection and sharing in the system. The consulting team can provide an experience base, but vehicles must be designed and incorporated into the organization to ensure the continuous performance of the function.

A second important integrating function that the consulting team can provide is the linking process between and among the alienated parts. For example, when two or more consultants have data which indicate difficulties in specific relationships among the suborganizational units with which they are working, then they can design and implement the action necessary to build more effective relationships. This was especially important in the illustrative case because the characteristic difficulties in the relationships among the MS functional departments were similar to the difficulties between MS and other groups in the organization.

The integrating function provided initially by the consulting team is very significant. One caution in this regard is that the members of the consulting team may very easily become identified with the departments they are working with. Differentiation and separateness may be appropriate early in the consulting team arrangement, but if they persist beyond the point at which integration must take place, the organization is hindered from achieving its full function and the consultants are not fulfilling their responsibilities. In a sense there is a degree of suboptimization that takes place; it is possible for each sub-organization to be "healthy" and yet the total organization may not be functioning as well as it could be.

Relationship to external consultants

There are situations in organizational life where having internal resources for change is not a luxury but a necessity. For the moment, let's begin with two statements that might be considered givens:

1) Most organizational change efforts initially employ, in some form, an external organizational consultant.

2) In most organizational change programs there is a useful and necessary function for the "change agent" role.

A significant part of the external consultant's strategy is, from the very beginning, explicit planning for the development of internal change agents. The specific method, of course, can vary. One way would be to involve several internal people in the change process at the outset and to train them to some degree of proficiency in the change agent role. Another approach would be to develop and implement a fairly comprehensive training program aimed specifically at the development of organizational consulting skills.

The degree to which a consulting team is able to apply its specialized resources effectively depends largely on how effective it is. Hence it may very well be worth the time and effort very early in the formation of a consulting team to build the kind of group in which resources are readily explored and inventoried, there is a developing commitment and willingness of team members to help one another with their consulting processes, and there is continuing trust building so that as much concrete data about their respective suborganizations can be shared as possible. At times then, the same kind of processes that the consulting team encourages its clients to engage in are also applicable to its own functioning as an organizational organism. This means that a continual assessment of the way in which the consultants are functioning as a team, the way in which they are using their resources, and the way in which they are proceeding with their consulting task is necessary. For this reason, it is useful for the consulting team to employ a consultant to assist it in its own team building activities and ongoing self-evaluation.

Sustaining the change effort

Very often the initial excitement, challenge, and impetus for change dissipates as the drudgery and hard work becomes more and more evident and necessary. It is difficult to maintain the "euphoric high," especially as other day-to-day activities impinge on the internal consulting team. The team can, and often must, provide the kind of reinforcement, support, and encouragement crucial to maintaining a level of energy required to sustain the change effort. Providing opportunities for new members to join the team and for others to "retreat" for brief periods sometimes contributes to the synergistic quality of the team's efforts.

SUMMARY

In this chapter some relevant dimensions of consultation were described and a model for the utilization of a consulting team was presented. An illustrative case was used to demonstrate the effective use of an internal consulting team to facilitate organizational change. Although there are issues that must be confronted and addressed if the team is to be a useful instrument, the approach offers the potential of providing an organization with a cadre capable both of performing the roles necessary for continual assessment of organizational performance and processes and of implementing changes necessary for improving organizational effectiveness. This internal capability of the organization can make its response to environmental needs and social demands much more resilient.

REFERENCES

Jacques, Eliot. "Social therapy: Technocracy or collaboration?" *Journal of Social Issues* 3 (Spring 1947): 59–66.

Lippitt, R., J. Watson, and B. Westerly. *Dynamics of Planned Change.* Harcourt Brace Jovanovich, Inc., 1958.

Margulies, N. "Implementing organizational change through the use of internal consulting teams." *Training and Development Journal* 25 (July 1971): 26–33.

Margulies, N., and Anthony P. Raia. "Action research and the consultative process." *Business Perspectives* 5 (Fall 1968): 26–30.

Some Concluding Propositions

10

In the course of this book we have examined the more important techniques for introducing planned and deliberate change in complex organizations. Our emphasis throughout has been upon the behavior of organizational members and our perspective that of applied behavioral science. For the manager concerned with the problems of organizational change, we have exposed the many technical alternatives available to him. Depending upon the constraints of his particular situation, he can choose among a wide variety of available techniques. Our book is intended to assist him in making informed and reasonable decisions about where and how to intervene in a complex social organization to produce effective change.

Implicit in our discussion of techniques have been several guiding propositions about the change process. Although several of these were made explicit at the outset, there is considerable value in stating them at the conclusion as well. In addition to providing the manager with a useful framework for approaching the process of change, these propositions may stimulate further thinking leading toward testable hypotheses.

Proposition 1. *Any change effort in which changes in individual behavior are required, regardless of initial focus, must include means for ensuring that such changes occur.*

Were it not for the fact that this obvious proposition is rather consistently ignored by both practitioners and theorists of organizational change, we would find it unnecessary. Academics may debate the relative worths of "structure versus people," "technology versus structure," "technology versus people," "people versus structure," etc., as the basic material to be changed, but such polarization can only be called unfortunate. It fails to grasp the reality of the *system* properties of complex organizations. Discussions of dichotomies in organizational change are, or should be, a part of our past and we should move on to more fruitful discussions of systemic features. From this perspective, changes in organizations can begin anywhere—in structure, in technology, or in people. In the final analysis, however, changes in the *behavior of the individuals who cause the organization to function* must occur. These necessary changes cannot be left to chance; they must be planned and developed even when they are not at the initial focus for change. Of what good is a changed production process if individual workers have not been retrained to make it function effectively? What benefits can possibly be expected from a change in administrative structure that requires smooth management behavior from persons who have never functioned in a team before?

While it is true that changes in structure or technology must be accompanied by planned "people" changes, we must not overlook the converse of this statement. Changes in an organization's people may also give rise to the necessity for planned changes in administrative structure, and even, perhaps, in technology. As people in an organization change, certain aspects of managerial behavior and administrative structure may change as well. For example, as values centering around participation and openness develop, administrative structures characterized by extreme position authority and secrecy may have to adapt. And while it is perhaps difficult to imagine how changes in persons might affect organizational technology, it is not impossible. We live in an age of intense alteration of human values. It is entirely conceivable that demands will be made both from within and from without to alter technological processes, especially those that continue to affect the human ecosystem and the general quality of life negatively.

Proposition 2. *Organizational change is more likely to be met with success when key management people initiate and support the change process.*

Planned change efforts must have the support and understanding of important management personnel if they are to proceed smoothly and produce important effects. While there are undoubtedly exceptions to this rule, it is generally true that planned change efforts without support from top management are at a great disadvantage.

There is simply no substitute for the positive boost that an informed and sophisticated management can provide.

Proposition 3. *Organizational change is best accomplished when persons likely to be affected by the change are brought into the process as soon as possible.*

Change is a threatening thing to many people. While there are, of course, numerous exemplary people who can adapt to nearly anything, the vast majority of us are merely human. We would not take it lightly if we were to arrive at work one morning and discover a whole new ball game. Nobody appreciates the *fait accompli* except the person who manages to pull it off. For the most part, sudden and unexpected change creates and intensifies *resistance* to change. Involving people early in the change process not only acclimates them to the idea of change but permits them to take a hand in those changes which are likely to affect their jobs, relationships, and personal satisfactions.

Proposition 4. *Successful change is not likely to occur following the single application of any technique.*

Changes in behavior require time and effort if they are to be incorporated as stabilized patterns of action. Repeated applications of the same technique will most likely prove necessary if new patterns of behavior are to be learned and performed consistently and reliably.

Proposition 5. *Successful change programs must rely upon informed and motivated persons within the organization if the results are to be maintained.*

External consultants are often useful to an organization in the preliminary stages of analysis, designing the program, and executing the initial efforts. Such resource persons, however, cannot be counted upon to sustain the organization's efforts over time. The business of the maintenance of change must fall to resource people *within* the organization. Such valuable internal resources do not develop by chance. These persons must be trained, developed, and given the same managerial legitimacy as other respected and valued members of the organization.

Proposition 6. *No single technique is optimal for all organizational problems, contexts, and objectives.*

There are no magic panaceas in the organizational change technique repertoire, and "shotgun therapy" (random application of a single presumably potent technique or of a combination of them) should most certainly be avoided. The problem, as we have tried to make very clear, is a management *decision* problem. One must match the technique to the need, the situation, the constraints, and the objectives. It is, for example, utterly foolish to attempt to apply the standard T-group to any and all organizational problems. As we have seen, each technique has a *range of effectiveness*. Each is therefore good for some purposes and irrelevant, even potentially destructive, for others.

Since the application of change techniques requires informed *managerial choice*, it is very clear that the effectiveness of any technique depends upon the quality of analysis that precedes its selection. As in any managerial decision, faulty and incomplete prior analysis will result in poor decisions and ultimately in ineffective action.

One final statement is in order. This concerns *means* versus *ends* in the application of the techniques we have described. Techniques such as team development, intergroup exercises, and laboratory training are *not* ends in and of themselves. They *are* means to reach clearly defined organizational change goals. It sometimes happens that managers, consultants, and organization members become so enamored with the intriguing world of personal development and interpersonal interaction represented in the techniques of change that they forget their original purposes. Management must monitor such techniques continuously to make certain that they remain in the service of organizational objectives and do not become ends in themselves.

With this discussion of some important propositions concerning change, we have completed our examination of the theory and techniques of organizational change. We began with a recognition of the forces both within and without the modern organization that call for a management sophisticated in the most recent developments in producing such change, but we must realize that the negative aspects of change are too often emphasized. Change is inevitable; it is a *natural process* and can be seen in the incessant flux of aging and evolution in all living systems. It need not, however, be seen as so troublesome, stressful, and, indeed, catastrophic as some regard it. Change must rightfully be regarded as the vital, creative, exciting, and energizing force that it really is. Planned organizational change is one way that this magnificent energy can be harnessed for the good of persons everywhere. The techniques we have described are the practical means by which this can be accomplished.

Index

Date Due
